THE FUNERAL SOURCEBOOK

Other Books by Dr. Lockyer . . .

All the Men of the Bible
All the Kings and Queens of the Bible
All the Prayers of the Bible
All the Promises of the Bible
All the Miracles of the Bible
All the Parables of the Bible
All the Doctrines of the Bible
All the Books and Chapters of the Bible
The Man Who Changed the World

THE
FUNERAL
SOURCEBOOK

by

Herbert Lockyer

ZONDERVAN PUBLISHING HOUSE

GRAND RAPIDS   MICHIGAN

Grateful acknowledgment is made to the
McGraw-Hill Book Company for permission to
reprint the five prayers found on pages
143-147, taken from *The Prayers
of Peter Marshall*, edited by Catherine
Marshall, Copyright 1954 by Catherine Marshall.

Printed in the United States of America

PREFACE

The author of this funeral manual is conscious of the fact that there are very many honored pastors who do not require such a tangible help. Age, and a long experience of caring for the dying, the dead, and the bereaved, have enabled them to formulate an effective approach of their own. Through constant contact with the sorrowing over many years, they have become most skillful in the art of consolation. However, in the compilation of this sourcebook for pastors in their funeral ministry, we had in mind the hundreds of theological students of all denominations who yearly enter the ministry, and will require guidance and assistance as they are called upon to speak with the dying, bury the dead, and comfort and advise the bereaved. While the newly ordained pastor will no doubt secure the manual covering all pastoral ministrations published by his own denomination, it is hoped that the more general and comprehensive one, herewith presented, will provide the young pastor with a wide coverage of material he can have at hand for use as required.

A man is not in the ministry long before he realizes what it means to be a servant of the Lord, both among the members of his own flock, as well as among those who profess no religious connection, yet seek his aid in times of stress and need. Sudden and frequent calls will make inroads upon the time he proposes to set aside for pulpit preparation, and he requires suitable material at hand enabling him to render inspiring and immediate service when death strikes a family in his church. It is to be hoped that with this book in hand the active pastor will find valuable materials in the form of sermons and Scripture selections, prayers and poems, etiquette and manner, enabling him to carry the Gospel of consolation to the distressed and broken-hearted in the hour of great sorrow. Grief and mourning cannot be disregarded or treated formally by any man who has the solemn responsibility of ministering to the souls of men. At all times, he must be at his best, and give of his best for God and man.

As a preparation for an effective ministry among the dying and the bereaved, pastors are warmly advised to acquaint themselves with literature designed to guide them in a right approach to the varied services they are called upon to render. Among works of worth they should peruse are —

> *The Art of Ministering to the Sick*, by Cabot and Dicks (Macmillan and Co., New York) 1956.
>
> *Death, Grief and Mourning*, by Geoffrey Gorer (Published by the Cresset Press, London).
>
> *A Grief Observed*, by C. S. Lewis (Published by Faber and Faber, London) 1960.
>
> *Pastoral Counselling*, by Seward Hiltner (Published by Abingdon Press, Nashville).
>
> *Understanding Grief*, by Edgar N. Jackson (Published by Abingdon Press, Nashville).
>
> *The Art of Dying*, by Herbert Lockyer (Published by Kregels, Grand Rapids, Mich.) 1966.
>
> *Christian Faith and Pastoral Care*, by Charles D. Kean (Published by Seabury Press, New York).
>
> *Widows and Their Families*, by Peter Marris (Published by Humanities Press, New York).
>
> *The Care of the Aged, the Dying, and the Dead*, by Alfred Worcester (Published by Charles C. Thomas, Springfield, Illinois).
>
> *Bereavement, Grief, and Mourning* (Published by the Clinical Theological Association, Nottingham, England).

Many standard works on "homiletics," such as *The Minister and His Ministry*, by Mark W. Lee, and published by the

Zondervan Publishing House, Grand Rapids, carry a chapter dealing with the pastor's responsibilities toward the dying, the dead and the bereaved. As his library will contain several volumes on professional guidance, the chapters devoted to "death" and "mourning" should be carefully read. Further, the pastor, eager to be well-equipped, is advised, not only to use the ministerial manual his own denomination publishes, but the manuals other religious bodies provide, as well as those compiled for general use as, for instance, that excellent *Pastor's Ideal Funeral Book*, by Arthur H. De Long.

At all times the faithful pastor will remember that he has been called to function as "the only man whom the Lord of the place whither thou art going hath authorized to be thy guide, in the difficult places thou mayest meet with in the way," as John Bunyan portrays the Interpreter of Scripture who must ever "bear his great commission in his look." One of the choicest portrayals of the ideal character and qualifications of a pastor is that which godly Bishop Ken gave the Church:

> Give me the priest whose graces shall possess
> Of an *Ambassador* the just address;
> A *father's* tenderness, a *shepherd's* care,
> A *leader's* courage, which the cross can bear,
> A *ruler's* awe, a *watchman's* wakeful life,
> A *fisher's* patience, and a *labourer's* toil;
> A *guide's* dexterity to disembroil;
> A *prophet's* inspiration from above;
> A *teacher's* knowledge, and a *Saviour's* love.

CONTENTS

Preface

Chapter 1

PASTORAL MINISTRATIONS

Before Death — Home and Hospital Visitation
At Death — Church and Committal Services
After Death — Spiritual and Practical Care;
     The Question of Cremation

Chapter 2 ˘

GUIDES FOR DIFFERENT FUNERALS

The Burial of an Aged Person
The Burial for a Middle-aged Person
The Burial of a Young Person
The Burial of a Child
The Burial of an Unknown Person
The Burial of a Suicide
The Burial of a Member of the Armed Forces
The Burial of a Distinguished Person in City or Nation
The Burial of a Company Suddenly Killed
Message for a Memorial Service

Chapter 3

SELECTED FUNERAL SERMONS

Sermon Outlines:
 Death Conquered
 The Christian's Prospect Beyond Death

Chapter 4

BENEFICIAL AIDS AND EXAMPLES 143

THE FUNERAL SOURCEBOOK

1

PASTORAL MINISTRATIONS

In this initial chapter we are to think of the deathbed ministry, funeral services, and the necessary after-care and consolation of the bereaved. Death in a family places the pastor in a strategic position as a spiritual counselor, and as a human paraclete between the God of comfort and the brokenhearted. There are no occasions when the man of God is more needed in a home than in the hour when death has laid its cold hand upon one of the family. It is then that, as a man, he is as a "covert from the tempest," and as "the shadow of a great rock in a weary land" (Isaiah 32:2).

Before Death

Learning of the sickness of one of his flock, the pastor knows that whether the person is at home, or in the hospital, that visitation is not only one of the most precious privileges of his ministry but likewise one of his most necessary tasks. To be of the utmost help in the hour of such need he must have, as well as the physician, a good bedside manner, which means that his dress should be somber, his bearing, serene and tender, and hopeful. His visit should be brief, and free from any appearance of haste; and he, himself, should appear quite natural and in no way professional or perfunctory. If the pastor senses that the sickness is fatal, or learns from his confidential co-operation with the family physician that the end is near, or hears from the stricken one that death approaches, then comes his precious opportunity of spiritual aid. Although visits to the dying should be brief, they should be used to the full to discover if the one appointed to die has the assurance of pardon and salvation.

If the dying one is a decided Christian and meets death not as a foe, but as a friend, then the pastor's task will be easy in the confirmation of the faith and confidence of the sufferer about to enter the valley of the shadow of death. But if, on the other hand, the stricken person is depressed because of unpreparedness for eternity, then the pastor must strive by the Spirit to lead the troubled soul into the joy of forgiveness and into rest in Christ. It sometimes happens that the person is not fully aware, as others are, that death is imminent. In such a circumstance the pastor needs heavenly wisdom to broach the matter of the patient's fatal illness in a way calculated to prepare him or her for the end. Often words of comfort and eternity fall on receptive ears, and a penitent trust in Christ ensues. Committing the dying one and the sorrowing members of the family to God in a few expressive sentences of prayer, the sympathetic and understanding pastor wins the confidence of the family. Occasionally visits have to be made to those suffering from contagious and infectious diseases. In his effort to spiritually assist those thus afflicted, the pastor should be careful not to break the laws regulating the isolation of infected persons, or expose himself unnecessarily. In close association with the physician, he must act as advised.

In these days of advanced medical knowledge and care, those who suffer from critical illnesses are removed to hospitals for expert treatment, and thus the pastor finds himself a frequent visitor at the local, or out-of-town hospital. As he walks through the wards, he will pass many who look lonely, discouraged and apprehensive, and his smile and salutation in passing lightens the load of the sufferers. If he learns from the doctors that the patient he is visiting will not recover from the accident, or cancerous trouble, or heart disease, or the operation recently performed, then it is the task of Christianity to aid such a doomed person to die nobly and with full assurance of life forevermore. It is the solemn responsibility of the pastor to apply the cordial of the Gospel and assure the dying that all is well if Christ is enshrined in the heart as Saviour and Lord. Care will be taken to remind the dying that the tragedy or triumph of death is in the way one dies, not in the act and fact of death itself. John Wesley said that his preachers died well, which they did, because theirs was the hope of a land of pure delight beyond this present vale of tears. The dying one can be reminded how Jesus faced both life and death in the Garden of Gethsemane when He prayed to the Father, "If it be possible, let this cup pass from me: nevertheless, not as I will, but as thou wilt" (Matthew 26:39). Attention can also be drawn to the fact that Paul's letters glow with light from a heart prepared for either life or death. "For to me to live is Christ, and to die is gain" (Philippians 1:21). He knew that if he lived, grace would be his to spread still further the good news of salvation among men; and that if he died, his departure would advance the faith for which he had lived and labored.

Suggested prayer for a person troubled in mind or in conscience and afraid to die:

"O Blessed Lord, the Father of mercies, and the God of all comforts: we beseech Thee, look down in pity and compassion upon this Thy afflicted servant. Thou writest bitter things against him (or her), and makest him (or her) to possess his (or her) former iniquities: Thy wrath lieth hard upon him (or her), and the soul is full of trouble. But, O merciful God who hast written Thy holy Word for our learning, that we through patience and comfort of Thy holy Scriptures, might have hope, give him (or her) a right understanding of himself (or herself), and of Thy threats and promises; that he (or she) may not cast away his (or her) confidence in Thee, nor place it anywhere but in Thee. Give strength against all temptations, and heal all distempers. Break not the bruised reed, nor quench the smoking flax. Shut not up Thy tender mercies in displeasure, but make him (or her) to hear joy and gladness, that the bones

Thou hast broken may rejoice. Deliver from the fear of the future, and lift up the light of Thy countenance upon him (or her), and give peace through the merits and mediation of Jesus Christ our Lord. *Amen.*

The following commendatory prayer for a person at the point of death is given in *The Book of Common Prayer*, as used by the Church of England ministers:

"O Almighty God, with whom do live the spirits of just men made perfect, after they are delivered from their earthly prisons: We humbly commend the soul of this Thy dear servant, our dear *brother* (or *sister*), into Thy hands, as into the hands of a faithful Creator, and most Merciful Saviour; most humbly beseeching Thee that it may be precious in Thy sight. Wash it, we pray Thee, in the blood of that immaculate Lamb, that was slain to take away the sins of the world; that whatsoever defilements it may have contracted in the midst of this miserable world, through the lusts of the flesh, or the wiles of Satan, being purged and done away, it may be presented pure and without spot before Thee. And teach us who survive, in this and other like daily spectacles of mortality, to see how frail and uncertain our condition is; and so to number our days, that we may seriously apply our hearts to that holy and heavenly wisdom, whilst we live here, which may in the end bring us to life everlasting, through the merits of Jesus Christ, Thine only Son our Lord. *Amen!*"

At Death

As soon as the "king of terrors" has struck, the gracious and sympathetic pastor can render varied, appreciable service. Experience has taught him a sensitiveness as to the requirements of the bereaved. First of all, by his quiet and tender demeanor he can comfort the grief-stricken, especially if they chide themselves that they had not cared or done enough for the deceased. Often the sorrowing feel that had they been more loving, kind and considerate, those they mourn would have lived longer.

While it is only too true that many do die in loneliness, neglected by their nearest relatives, the pastor, whether by his knowledge of the family, or intuition, will know how to meet such a sentiment. When there are pent-up feelings, and he realizes that a good cry would be a relief, the pastor will be ready to tell the fatigued, dumb-stricken sufferers to let their hearts feel their sorrow, and to allow their tears to flow. Comfortable words of Scripture will come to his remembrance to uplift the distressed. "Speak ye comfortably to my people."

The reason why pastors are so continuously involved in the consolation of the bereaved, and the disposal of the dead, is because Christianity is dogmatic that the soul continues to exist after death, and faces judgment. "After death, the judgment" (Hebrews 9:27). The hope and belief that the departed are in eternal bliss comforts the bereaved, while the fear of future condemnation warns sinners of the eternity awaiting them if they die in their sin.

As soon as death appears, the ministrations of the pastor can be of a very necessary and practical nature. He can advise about funeral arrangements, public announcements, and the claiming of insurances, or compensation, if the lamented one was killed. Where a pastor is deeply attached to a family, he will be relied upon to advise the relatives of the deceased on matters requiring immediate attention. Because of the high efficiency of modern funeral directors, everything associated with funeral etiquette and ceremonies is cared for. Their service includes the securing of the death certificate and burial permit, notification of coroner or medical examiner in the case of accidental or violent death; placement of obituary notices, arrangement for transportation if the body is to be buried away from the point of death; decision as to time, place, and services for funeral with the security of an officiating minister if the family of the deceased is not connected with any local church; receiving, acknowledging, and recording all condolences and flowers; caring for necessary cemetery space, and for any desired military or fraternal ceremonies.

Although the funeral business, like other businesses, has

gathered a few unscrupulous practitioners, as the exposé found in the much-discussed volume, *The American Way of Death*, by Jessica Mitford clearly reveals, yet on the whole funeral directors, like faithful pastors, are conscious of the spiritual import of their task and serve the bereaved in a wonderful way without excessive gain. The pastor can be relied upon to counsel the sorrowing who want to pay their best respect to the dead, not to beggar themselves by an expensive funeral. He is in an ideal position to assure the next of kin what is proper in the equipment of the funeral. In cases where the cleaning of homes has been neglected because of long sickness before death, the pastor can marshall members of his church to undertake many duties calculated to relieve the bereaved, and prepare the home if the funeral service is to be held there. Where there has been no spiritual or continuing relationship between a pastor and a home, many nonreligious people still feel that when death occurs a minister must be secured to conduct the funeral, just as the undertaker is hired to do his job. Yet even in such cases the pastor, eager for opportunities for witness, will readily serve if called upon and use the event to press home the necessity of preparation to meet God.

As the majority of people die in their own bed or in a hospital ward, and the funeral service takes place in the home, or church, or funeral chapel or cemetery chapel, the young inexperienced pastor, eager to fulfill commendably the task of burying the dead, has before him a clear understanding of the aspects of burial and committal aspects of the occasion, and the most fitting Scriptures, hymns, prayers and messages so that the funeral as a whole will redound to God's glory in the comfort and edification of all assembled. As the pastor is alone responsible for the entire religious aspects of the funeral, it is essential for him to have everything so perfectly in hand that there will be no hitch or delay of any kind. If the burial service is to be held in the home of the deceased, then it will be brief seeing that hymn singing and the usual church order of service may not be possible. In such a close capacity with relatives and friends of the family around him, the pastor will be able to speak in a subdued, conversational way, of the matters of eternal significance, and prayerfully express the feelings and hopes of the bereaved. The writer can testify to having participated in many impressive home funeral services.

Usually, however, in these modern times with the development of funeral homes with their mortuaries, the dead are removed and prepared for burial, and the funeral service held in a church, or a cemetery chapel. When the service is held in the church, the pastor may be requested to go to the house of mourning for a brief reading of Scripture and prayer and then accompany the bereaved to the house of God. Reaching it, the pastor stands at the door and then leads the cortège down the aisle reciting in a clear and distinct voice such passages as the following:

"I am the resurrection, and the life, he that believeth in me, though he were dead, yet shall he live: And whosoever liveth and believeth in me shall never die."

John 11:25, 26

* * *

"I know that my Redeemer liveth, and that he shall stand at the latter day upon the earth. And though after my skin worms destroy this body, yet in my flesh shall I see God: Whom I shall see for myself, and mine eyes shall behold, and not another."

Job 19:25-27

* * *

"We brought nothing into this world, and it is certain we can carry nothing out. The Lord gave, and the Lord hath taken away; blessed be the name of the Lord."

I Timothy 6:7; Job 1:21

When the casket is rested and the pallbearers have either retired or seated themselves, the pastor is then ready to commence the burial service which should not exceed thirty to forty-five minutes. As funeral addresses are becoming more or less obsolete, and brief, tender words of honorable eulogy and a few sentences of guidance and cheer have taken their place, services are shorter. But where there is a longer service it might take the order of —

A Brief Invocation
A Suitable Hymn
The Prayer
Selected Scriptures
Short Message
A Hymn
The Benedication.

From the Psalms the following make impressive reading:

I said, I will take heed to my ways, that I sin not with my tongue: I will keep my mouth with a bridle, while the wicked is before me.

I was dumb with silence, I held my peace, even from good: and my sorrow was stirred.

My heart was hot within me, while I was musing the fire burned: then spake I with my tongue,

Lord, make me to know mine end, and the measure of my days, what it is; that I may know how frail I am.

Behold, thou hast made my days as an handbreadth; and mine age is as nothing before thee: verily every man at his best state is altogether vanity. Selah.

Surely every man walketh in a vain shew: surely they are disquieted in vain: he heapeth up riches, and knoweth not who shall gather them.

And now, Lord, what wait I for? my hope is in thee. Deliver me from all my transgressions: make me not the reproach of the foolish.

I was dumb, I opened not my mouth; because thou didst it.

Remove thy stroke away from me: I am consumed by the blow of thine hand.

When thou with rebukes dost correct man for iniquity, thou makest his beauty to consume away like a moth: surely every man is vanity. Selah.

Hear my prayer, O Lord, and give ear unto my cry; hold not thy peace at my tears: for I am a stranger with thee, and a sojourner, as all my fathers were.

O spare me, that I may recover strength, before I go hence, and be no more.

Psalm 39

* * *

Lord, thou hast been our dwelling place in all generations.

Before the mountains were brought forth, or ever thou hadst formed the earth and the world, even from everlasting to everlasting, thou art God.

Thou turnest man to destruction; and sayest, Return, ye children of men.

For a thousand years in thy sight are but as yesterday when it is past, and as a watch in the night.

Thou carriest them away as with a flood; they are as a sleep: in the morning they are like grass which groweth up.

In the morning it flourisheth, and groweth up; in the evening it is cut down, and withereth.

For we are consumed by thine anger, and by thy wrath are we troubled.

Thou hast set our iniquities before thee, our secret sins in the light of thy countenance.

For all our days are passed away in thy wrath: we spend our years as a tale that is told.

The days of our years are threescore years and ten; and if by reason of strength they be fourscore years, yet is there strength labour and sorrow; for it is soon cut off, and we fly away.

Who knoweth the power of thine anger? even according to thy fear, so is thy wrath.

So teach us to number our days, that we may apply our hearts unto wisdom.

Return, O Lord, how long? and let it repent thee concerning thy servants.

O satisfy us early with thy mercy; that we may rejoice and be glad all our days.

Make us glad according to the days wherein thou hast afflicted us, and the years wherein we have seen evil.

Let thy work appear unto thy servants, and thy glory unto their children.

And let the beauty of the Lord our God be upon us: and establish thou the work of our hands upon us; yea, the work of our hands establish thou it.

Psalm 90

* * *

From Paul's first Corinthian letter we read:

But now is Christ risen from the dead, and become the firstfruits of them that slept.

For since by man came death, by man came also the resurrection of the dead.

For as in Adam all die, even so in Christ shall all be made alive.

But every man in his own order: Christ the firstfruits; afterward they that are Christ's at his coming.

Then cometh the end, when he shall have delivered up the kingdom to God, even the Father; when he shall have put down all rule and all authority and power.

For he must reign, till he hath put all enemies under his feet.

The last enemy that shall be destroyed is death.

For he hath put all things under his feet. But when he saith all things are put under him, it is manifest that he is excepted, which did put all things under him.

And when all things shall be subdued unto him, then shall the Son also himself be subject unto him that put all things under him, that God may be all in all.

Else what shall they do which are baptized for the dead, if the dead rise not at all? why are they then baptized for the dead?

And why stand we in jeopardy every hour?

I protest by your rejoicing which I have in Christ Jesus our Lord, I die daily.

If after the manner of men I have fought with beasts at Ephesus, what advantageth it me, if the dead rise not? let us eat and drink; for tomorrow we die.

Be not deceived; evil communications corrupt good manners.

Awake to righteousness, and sin not; for some have not the knowledge of God: I speak this to your shame.

But some man will say, How are the dead raised up? and with what body do they come?

Thou fool, that which thou sowest is not quickened, except it die:

And that which thou sowest, thou sowest not that body that shall be, but bare grain, it may chance of wheat, or of some other grain:

But God giveth it a body as it hath pleased him, and to every seed his own body.

All flesh is not the same flesh: but there is one kind of flesh of men, another flesh of beasts, another of fishes, and another of birds.

There are also celestial bodies, and bodies terrestrial: but the glory of the celestial is one, and the glory of the terrestrial is another.

There is one glory of the sun, and another glory of the moon, and another glory of the stars: for one star differeth from another star in glory.

So also is the resurrection of the dead. It is sown in corruption; it is raised in incorruption:

It is sown in dishonour; it is raised in glory: it is sown in weakness; it is raised in power:

It is sown a natural body; it is raised a spiritual body. There is a natural body, and there is a spiritual body.

And so it is written, The first man Adam was made a living soul; the last Adam was made a quickening spirit. Howbeit that was not first which is spiritual, but that which is natural; and afterward that which is spiritual. The first man is of the earth, earthy: the second man is the Lord from heaven.

As is the earthy, such are they also that are earthy: and as is the heavenly, such are they also that are heavenly.

And as we have borne the image of the earthy, we shall also bear the image of the heavenly.

Now this I say, brethren, that flesh and blood cannot inherit the kingdom of God; neither doth corruption inherit incorruption.

Behold, I shew you a mystery; We shall not all sleep, but we shall all be changed,

In a moment, in the twinkling of an eye, at the last trump: for the trumpet shall sound, and the dead shall be raised incorruptible, and we shall be changed. For this corruptible must put on incorruption, and this mortal must put on immortality.

So when this corruptible shall have put on incorruption, and this mortal shall have put on immortality, then shall be brought to pass the saying that is written, Death is swallowed up in victory.

O death, where is thy sting? O grave, where is thy victory?

The sting of death is sin; and the strength of sin is the law.

But thanks be to God, which giveth us the victory through our Lord Jesus Christ.

Therefore, my beloved brethren, be ye stedfast, unmoveable, always abounding in the work of the Lord, forasmuch as ye know that your labour is not in vain in the Lord.

I Corinthians 15:20-58

* * *

Other appropriate Scriptures are Psalms 23, 46, 103; John 14; Romans 8; II Corinthians 5:1-10; I Thessalonians 4:13-18; Revelation 7:9-17; 21; 22.

As for the prayer, it should not be designed to stir the emotions of those assembled but inspire quietness and peace of mind. While it must contain a reference to the deceased, and present the needs of the sorrowing circle of relatives and friends, the intercession should express confession of conscious unworthiness and gratitude to God for eternal life through Christ. A pastor must never be guilty of preaching at the people through his prayer. The Lord's Prayer can follow the pastor's prayer, seeing it is a family prayer.

If a sermon is given it should embrace these three features: recognition of the deceased, comfort for the bereaved and warning for those who are not ready for the "Great Beyond." Guides as to appropriate messages can be found in our section dealing with Funeral Sermons. The pastor must endeavor to give the service a simple dignity and impressiveness. The service ended, the pastor heads the mourners, as the casket leaves the church, and follows the same order when the cemetery is reached. At the graveside, the pastor takes a position at the best vantage point so that all can see and hear him. If the weather is very wet, cold and wintry, male mourners should be advised not to uncover their heads. The committal ceremony should be brief, consisting of a few passages of Scripture, prayer and benediction. Thereafter the pastor should shake hands with the nearest of kin and leave with them a word of spiritual comfort. Often relatives feel the strain of such a farewell and are distraught, and require the sympathetic word of the pastor. We herewith append suggestions as to Scripture verses and prayer for use at the graveside, as well as an order of the actual committal.

"Man that is born of a woman hath but a short time to live, and is full of misery: He cometh up, and is cut down, like a flower; he fleeth as it were a shadow, and never continued in one stay.

In the midst of life we are in death: of whom may we seek succour, but of thee, O Lord, who for our sins art justly displeased? Yet, O Lord God most holy, O Lord most mighty, O holy and most merciful Saviour, deliver us not into the pains of eternal death. Thou knowest, Lord, the secrets of our hearts; shut not thy merciful ears to our prayer; but spare us, Lord most holy, O God most mighty, O holy and merciful Saviour, thou most worthy Judge

eternal, suffer us not at our last hour, for any pains of
death, to fall from thee."

As the body is lowered into the grave, it is the custom with
some pastors to take up a little of the earth or a few flowers
or sprigs of evergreen and drop them into the grave as they
repeat a committal formula. Different denominations provide
their pastors with their own particular funeral manual, and
these contain varying commital sentences. Ministers of the
Anglican Church say —

> "Forasmuch as it hath pleased Almighty God of His great
> mercy to take unto Himself the soul of our dear brother
> (or sister) here departed: we therefore commit his (or
> her) body to the ground; earth to earth, ashes to ashes,
> dust to dust; in the sure and certain hope of the Resurrection
> to eternal life, through our Lord Jesus Christ; who shall
> change the body of our humiliation, that it may be like unto
> His glorious body, according to the mighty working, whereby
> He is able to subdue all things to Himself."

* * *

A brief portion of Scripture, such as Revelation 14:13 can then
be quoted:

> "I heard a voice from heaven saying unto me, Write,
> Blessed are the dead which die in the Lord from hence-
> forth: Yea, saith the Spirit, that they may rest from their
> labours."

* * *

For a concluding prayer several final petitions have been suggested. Sometimes the Lord's Prayer is recited:

> "Our Father which art in heaven, Hallowed be thy name.
> Thy kingdom come. Thy will be done in earth, as it is
> in heaven.
> Give us this day our daily bread.
> And forgive us our debts, as we forgive our debtors.
> And lead us not into temptation, but deliver us from evil:

For thine is the kingdom, and the power, and the glory, for ever." *Amen*

Anglican ministers repeat —

"Almighty God, with whom do live the spirits of them that depart hence in the Lord, and with whom the souls of the faithful, after they are delivered from the burden of the flesh, are in joy and felicity: We give thee hearty thanks, for that it hath pleased thee to deliver this our brother (or sister) out of the miseries of this sinful world: beseeching thee that it may please thee, of thy gracious goodness, shortly to accompany the number of thine elect, and to hasten thy kingdom; that we, with all those that are departed in the true faith of the holy Name, may have our perfect comsummation and bliss, both in body and soul, in thy eternal and everlasting glory; through Jesus Christ our Lord.

The grace of our Lord Jesus Christ, and the love of God, and the fellowship of the Holy Spirit be with us all evermore." *Amen*

* * *

Among practical aspects of funeral arrangements we might consider, the first is the question of a fee for services rendered. Dealing with "Funeral Etiquette," Arthur H. De Long has the footnote —

"A minister should make no charges for his services other than his personal expenses; but where a fee is *tendered* there is no impropriety in his accepting it as a *gift* of appreciation, provided the family is in comfortable circumstances."

As the servant of the Lord and of needy hearts, a pastor should expect no recompense other than the assurance of having ministered comfort and hope to grief-stricken hearts. Privilege and duty are inherent in his call to the ministry. The custom has developed among funeral directors or undertakers to include the minister's burial fee in the over-all charge for a funeral, and hand him a check accordingly. Such a method saves a pastor the embarrassment of having to receive, direct from the bereaved relatives, any money for his services.

Another matter that sometimes arises is the request to have a former pastor come and bury a church member. Possibly he was the means of leading the deceased to Christ, or had a peculiar interest in the family and, because of a close attachment, the desire is expressed to have him conduct the funeral service. Graciously, of course, the present pastor welcomes such a wish, and cooperates in the former pastor's arrangements. It has been known, however, for a family to ignore the right of a present pastor to bury the father of the home who died, because of a strong antagonism to his spiritual ministry, and without consultation with the pastor, secure the previous less orthodox minister to return and conduct the funeral. Such an action is most unethical, but the understanding pastor should take it all with good grace, and may join the assembled company at the house-funeral as a mourner. Carnal-minded church members can cause a faithful pastor many a heartache, but he soon learns that every experience is worth what it costs.

A further feeling a pastor must guard against in funeral ministry is that of mere professionalism. His constant contact with the dying and the dead, may all unconsciously develop into a mechanical, cold-hearted conduct of a funeral service. At all times, it is necessary for him to have a tender, sympathetic and comforting attitude if his ministry in such a sad hour for others is to be effective. Neither will he yield to the modern effort to cover up the reality of death. Enterprising funeral directors strive to treat death as something foreign to man. The remains of the deceased are placed in a "slumber parlour," and the last rites are robbed of their grim existence by quiet music, quieter thick carpets, elaborate floral surroundings and the corpse embalmed, and all dressed up as if death had not taken place. In fact, in England, it is now becoming the custom not to mention the deceased's name at the Communion service on the Sunday following the funeral because its repetition would remind the family of their loss. But it is the solemn obligation of a pastor to remind people of the hard fact of death; that life still is transitory; that our loved ones do die and that their passing is often an overwhelming sorrow leaving a void that only reunion in heaven can fill. Because he lives in a world of sin and death, the pastor must ever confirm the voice of Scripture that, "It is appointed unto men once to die, but after this the judgment" (Hebrews 9:27).

After Death

The pastor's responsibility does not end with the benediction at the graveside. It is to his discredit if the mourners are compelled to say, "We have not seen the minister since the funeral." Usually the bereaved gather in the home of the deceased, with relatives and friends from far and near and meeting in a body exchange condolences and in some cases gather to hear the last will and testament read. If invited to return to the house, the pastor should accept, for in such a gathering of relatives, friends and neighbors, he will have an opportunity of prayer and witness. Hearts solemnized by the death and burial of the member of the household are open to the spiritual ministrations of the faithful pastor.

If the pastor has been diligent in the visitation of the dying, there will be a realization of what the family as a whole have had to face in anxious days and sleepless nights, and how when the end came, too often the nerves of the bereaved were taut as the result of the strain of mingled hope and fear. Often when the funeral is over the sorrowing are exhausted, numbed and emotionally intense, and the sympathetic pastor skilled in the art of consolation, can do much to ease their burden. A kind and understanding attitude greatly helps to soothe the grief-stricken when the vigil is over. As it is very rare for the dead to be buried without the service of a minister and religious rites, the Christ-possessed pastor, because of his constant contact with sorrow and his personal experience of death, has a Christian faith and a familiarity with the healing balm of Scripture with which he can serve the bereaved most effectively.

After the funeral, therefore, several visits must be paid to the shadowed home with its vacant seat, and every effort made to reduce the burden of grief. In his heart-moving volume on *The Passion for Souls*, Dr. J. H. Jowett speaks of "the ministry of the bleeding heart," and affirms that a preacher can only bless if he has bled. The words, "bleed" and "bless" come from the same root, the implication being that we can only bless as we bleed. Pastors with a Calvary heart know instinctively how to comfort those who have buried their dead, and sigh for the touch of the vanished hand. Such men of God, who have known what it is to bury half of their heart in a grave, are best fitted to work with Him who died and rose again, in the healing of the brokenhearted. Fellowship with the Man of Sorrows who became acquainted with human grief enables the faithful shepherd of souls to exercise an abiding spiritual influence in his ministry among the bereaved.

If, in the course of visitation well after the day of the funeral, heavy sorrow lingers, the judicious pastor will not condemn such continued sorrow. To do so would be to condemn love at a time when it needs spiritual reinforcement. Saints sorrow over the separation death brings, but not as those who have no hope (I Thessalonians 4:13, 14). Neither will the pastor err in offering false consolation by telling the bereaved to dry their tears and that before long they will feel differently. The spiritual comforter will remember and soothe an empty heart by saying that, "A love forgotten is a love dead, and that while love lives there will be suffering as well as joy." It is sheer folly to try to cheer up the sorrowing by saying that time is a great healer and that the world soon forgets its grief. Sorrow, not of the hopeless kind, is an evidence of faithfulness to the dead, and those who have lost their loved one are consoled as the pastor reminds them that in Christ they have their beloved dead forever. Attention will be drawn to the fact that although robbed of the actual presence of the departed, they have a harvest of memory.

During his post-funeral visits, the pastor may find those who were closely related to the dead, somewhat rebellious against God for the removal of one who was so necessary and much loved. Tenderly, the embittered heart must be led to submit to the mysterious but gracious will of God who never takes a wrong turning. If the pastor finds those of the deceased's family remorseful because of real or imagined unkindness or neglect, they must be reminded that tears and regret cannot make amends, and that they should give themselves to increased love and service toward the living. Sometimes the pastor will meet those whose grief is still more poignant because of their fear that the loved one who was taken made no profession of faith and was not prepared to die. As a faithful counselor, the pastor will not compromise with truth, but assure the anxious that we do not know what passes between God and the dying and that we can safely leave those who die to the unknown mercies of a loving God. One of the surprises of heaven will be the presence of those we least expected to be there. The pastor cannot explain the dark mysteries of providence, but he can correct the mistaken notion that an unexpected death came as divine punishment. Death is an *appointment* all must keep. Comforting passages of Scripture and a heartfelt prayer, never fail to leave stricken hearts with a consciousness of the presence and love of God, whose goodness faileth never. Such a spiritual ministry creates a calm assessment of death and of the life beyond.

Often the bereaved are too prostrate to take the initiative in legal matters concerning the dead one's estate, or claim any pensionable or compensation benefits, and it is here that the pastor can help in a most practical way those who have no clear perception what to do next. It is not easy to adjust oneself to altered circumstances, but when a wise, kind counselor is at hand to suggest and advise, the sorrowing take heart, and soon find an even keel. Because women frequently live longer than men, and widows become still more numerous, especially when war ravages the earth or disaster strikes, the Christian care of widows, the fatherless and orphans becomes the vital concern of a pastor and of the church he serves. From early Bible days divine instructions were clear as to provision for widows, or *silent ones* as the Hebrew word suggests. The fatherless and widows were the direct concern of God, hence the repetition of sympathetic references to widows by Old Testament prophets, and by Christ and His apostles. The office of deacon owes its origin to the Church's interest in the welfare of widows. It was because few troubled about these women who were particularly helpless that God reckoned them to be His special concern (Psalms 68:5; 146:9). To show kindness toward widows was to qualify for God's approach and blessing (Job 29:13; Isaiah 1:17; Jeremiah 7:6). Worthy widows must be honored (I Timothy 5:3), relieved by friends (I Timothy 5:4, 16), visited in time of need (James 1:27), and provided for by the Church (Acts 6:1; I Timothy 5:9).

Where help is required, the pastor is under the obligation of instituting some system of relief for those of his flock widowed by death. Guidance as to the way of taking advantage of charitable funds must be given, and to the possibility of obtaining suitable employment, as well as to the education of any fatherless, dependent children. In many practical ways the pastor can assist a woman, bereft of the breadwinner, to take up the threads of life again, and by doing so soften the blow sustained and encourage trust in the God who offers Himself as a Husband to the widow, and as a Father to the fatherless.

THE QUESTION OF CREMATION

Although this method of disposing of the dead is becoming increasingly popular, cremation is a divided question among Christians. While Dr. Charles R. Erdman in his volume, *The Work of the Pastor* says, "A pastor need not refuse to officiate at a cremation if given sufficient liberty as to the character of the religious service," the fact remains that many conscientious pastors feel they cannot officiate at a crematorium service. There is, of course, in the law governing cremation a clause which expressly exempts any minister from the obligation of performing a burial service either after or at a cremation. It is, therefore, for the guidance of the pastor that we set forth the pros and cons of cremation in order that we may know how to act more intelligently when any of his flock seek advice on this form of burial. Cremate, meaning "to burn," is allied to the Hebrew word Joshua used in connection with Achan the trespasser,

"He that is taken with the accursed thing shall be *burnt with fire,* he and all that he hath" (7:15). It is also akin to the Greek term Paul employs when he speaks about giving his body to be burned (I Corinthians 15:3).

As to the origin of cremation, turning back the pages of history we find that such a method of disposing of the dead was the general practice of the ancient, heathen world. From earliest times there have been various customs of burial, such as embalming, cremation, or exposure of the body to beasts and birds of prey. Cremation is supposed to have originated among the Aryans, whose discovery of fire lifted them above other races. Having a great veneration for fire these Aryans not only gathered around their camp fires but used it to dispose of their dead. Their folklore is replete with reference to the funeral pyres of their heroes. Invading armies would reduce the corpses of fallen warriors to ashes and return them to sorrowing relatives. Nomadic tribes practiced cremation and carried cinerary urns containing the ashes of their loved ones with them in their wanderings. The funeral pyre is said to have originated in ancient India among the Aryans, and cremation is still the national custom of burial in India among the Hindus, and is incorporated in their religion. Cinerary urns have been found on the wild steppes of Russia and in Scandinavian countries.

In Athens, during the height of her glory, and in the last days of the Roman Empire, cremation was practically the universal custom. The Greeks wove beautiful fancies around the rite, and believed that fire crested every living thing and that to free the soul from the bonds of matter, the body must be reduced to its original elements by flame. The Romans, absorbing Greek ideals along with their culture, practiced urn burial as well as earth burial. Cicero, however, held that earth burial was the more ancient practice. Because of the abuse of most extravagant funeral pyres, when Charlemagne came to power around A.D. 800, acting upon the edict of the Roman Church, he outlawed cremation. But such a custom was so deeply rooted among the Saxons, that to suppress it, the death penalty was instituted as a punishment for its practice. *The Encyclopaedia*

Britannica says that, "There can be no doubt that the practice of cremation in Europe was at the first stopped, and then prevented, in great measure, by the Christian doctrine of the resurrection of the body, partly also by the notion that the Christian body was redeemed and purified."

Coming to the Scriptural practice of burial, it is clear that both Jewish and Christian forms of the disposal of the dead was that of earth burial, and not cremation. The judgment upon Adam and Eve for their transgression indicates earth burial, "Dust thou art, and unto dust shalt thou return" (Genesis 3:19). Abraham, founder and father of the Jewish race, arranged for the burial of Sarah his wife (Genesis 15:13; 25). Egypt, persecutor of God's ancient people, practiced embalming. Then we have the detailed account of the death and burial of Moses (Deuteronomy 34:5, 6). Did the prohibitions concerning fire, include the burning of the body? (Leviticus 18:24; 20:1-4; Jeremiah 7:31, 32; Ezekiel 23:27). The latter references suggest that cremation was associated with special judgment. Joseph was embalmed and buried (Exodus 13:19; Joshua 24:32). There are two places in the Old Testament where cremation is mentioned without criticism. First, the bodies of Saul and his sons, so badly mangled, were burned before burial (I Samuel 31:12, 13). Then Amos refers to the burning of a man's kinsman, probably in time of plague (6:10). Earth burial made possible the miracle at Elisha's tomb (II Kings 13:21). The "very great burning" at the burial of Asa was not that of cremation but a burning of spices and furniture in the king's honor (II Chronicles 16:14, See Jeremiah 34:5). The prophecy against Jeroboam's false altar (I Kings 13:1-3) is simply a prophecy of a king who shall take the bones of those previously buried and the priests of the high places that burn incense in false worship and cause them to be burned on the false altar to further pollute it and render it abominable.

In the New Testament there is no actual reference to cremation. It is clearly evident that the early Christians followed the Jewish custom of earth burial. John reminds us that it was "the manner of the Jews to bury" (19:40). Jewish ritual, however, is silent in regard to specific methods of caring for the dead. When

Paul spoke of giving his body to be burned he was simply accommodating his language to the customs of Corinth. In his "Magna Carta of the Resurrection," the apostle speaks of "the sowing of the body" (I Corinthians 15:34-44). It is altogether beside the point to argue that because Jesus was buried in a grave, it is incumbent upon all His followers to be disposed of in the same way when they die. In the first place, the corpse of Jesus was not buried in a hole in the ground and covered over with a load of earth. He was buried in a rock-hewn vault prepared by wealthy Joseph of Arimathaea for himself (Matthew 27:57-61). Within this "new tomb hewn out of the rock," the body of Jesus lay on a slab of stone. Further, it was necessary for Jesus to be buried thus because it had been divinely decreed that He should rise the third day without any corruption having taken place in His body (Psalm 16:10; Acts 2:27, 31; 13:35). Had His body remained another day in the tomb, corruption and decomposition would have set in, for according to Martha's description of her much-loved brother, Lazarus, he had been been dead *four days* and began to stink (John 11:39). Jesus, therefore, came forth from the tomb with the very same body the disciples had washed and perfumed with spices — uncontaminated by corruption or decay; and it is that very body, withal glorified, that He has in heaven, and which we are to behold with awe.

The revival of cremation goes back to 1869, when the Italian scientist, Brunetti, devised a modern type of cremation which modern science has improved and brought to perfection, especially in America, where there are now some 300 crematoriums in use. The first white man to be cremated in America was Colonel Henry Laurens, president of the Continental Congress (1777-78), whose cremation took place according to his last will and testament on his estate in Charleston, S.C. Dr. William Temple was the first archbishop in England to be cremated which took place at Charing Crematorium, Kent, on October 31, 1944. Dr. G. Campbell Morgan, the renowned Bible expositor, was cremated, as was Dr. W. E. Sangster, the well-known Methodist leader. The late Lord Horder, one-time Court Physician and President of The Cremation Society of Great Britain, wrote —

"We regard cremation as a much-needed reform and as an essential public service — the most hygienic method. Cremation — an indoor service — safeguards the health of the mourner, whose health resistance may have been reduced by long periods of anxiety and vigil at the sick bed. Cremation induces a more rational attitude to death by eliminating the grave and the morbid atmosphere of the cemetery."

Francis E. Willard, the American educator and reformer once said, "Let no friend of mine say ought to prevent the cremation of my cast-off body." Ella Wheeler Wilcox likewise affirmed in an article on this matter—

"I heartily approve of Cremation. In the first place it is cleanly, it helps along nature; in the second place, it is economical. The body must eventually turn to dust. Why not by Cremation rather than have it decompose in the ground?"

Facing the fact that cremation is making rapid strides, the pastor may be constrained to ask whether anything more than a custom is involved, or whether there is some spiritual issue at stake. He may personally shrink from the idea of cremation, yet feel that it is not right to object to it. Perhaps he cannot give any cogent argument why he should not officiate at a crematorium. What he must bear in mind is that the Bible does not contain any judgment against the Greek and Roman practices of cremation in the same way as it warns against idolatry. Therefore, if modern crowded conditions make the availability of ground for cemeteries increasingly difficult, no Christian reason can be given against cremation as an expediency.

While unbelievers may sometimes practice cremation as a token of open defiance of God and the rejection of the truth of the resurrection of the body — which probably was the reason why the pronounced agnostic, George Bernard Shaw willed to be cremated — this does not nullify the decision regarding this mode of burial by Christians. What must be borne in mind is that the manner of burial makes no difference whatever to the resurrection. The actual burning of the body cannot bring any loss, otherwise the martyrs who suffered death by fire and Christians burned to death accidentally, or pulverized by an explosion, or eaten by wild animals or sharks at sea could be in a state of inferiority. After death, what happens to the body of the believer is of little consequence; it is the joy of resurrection that counts (Job 19:25-27; Philippians 3:21). The Earl of Shaftesbury, the great reformer, once asked, "What will become of the blessed martyrs if the body cannot be returning to God in its original form by a wise and just God? The ashes of a saint are truly as venerable as his bones."

Both the Bible and science confirm that "dust we are and unto dust we shall return." If the body is buried in a grave, the human body slowly disintegrates into the basic molecules of which it is composed. Whether this breakdown occurs rapidly, as in cremation, or slowly as in an ordinary burial appears immaterial. We are not to think of our blessed dead as dust or ashes, but as absent from the body and present with the Lord. God knows how He will gather the dust or ashes together when the miracle of resurrection takes place. Cremation is not inconsistent with the Christian doctrine of resurrection. Having the power to resurrect, God can bring forth resurrected bodies from buried dust or ashes. Did not Jesus say that God is able to raise up children to Abraham out of the stones, and what is a stone, but solidified dust? There is no argument at all in saying that to be forced to be burned as the martyrs were is one thing, but to deliberately plan cremation is another matter. There is nothing anti-Christian about such a form of burial. Therefore, if a pastor is requested to officiate at a crematorium, he should respect the freedom of the individual conscience, if he can offer no Scriptural evidence against cremation, or present any specific command condemning it.

While cremation has never been universally popular among Christians, and is not likely to become the prevailing practice in Christendom in our generation, and pastors may find that the majority of people feel it better to follow the custom and give their dead a decent burial, the fact remains that cremation is more hygienic and economical, and easier on the bereaved. The ultimate choice, then, is between earth burial, where nature takes her slow and painful course of disintegration, or the higher method of science for reducing dust to dust and ashes to ashes. Clean, purifying heat accomplishes in a short time what nature, unaided, takes years to bring about. If cremation offers a more loving deference to the departed, and greater consideration for future generations, then the wise pastor cannot refuse to serve those who wish it, even though the moment the casket disappears through the folding doors in the crematorium chapel is one of most poignant finality.

SUPPLEMENTARY READINGS

Erdman, Charles *The Work of the Pastor*, (Westminster Press, Philadelphia) 1924

Gorer, Geoffrey *Death, Grief and Mourning*, (Cresset Press, London)

Hiltner, Seward *Pastoral Counselling*, (Abingdon Press, Nashville)

Jackson, Edgar *Understanding Grief*, (Abingdon Press, Nashville)

Jowett, Dr. J. H. *The Passion for Souls*

Kean, Charles D. *Christian Faith and Pastoral Care*, (Seabury Press, New York)

Marris, Peter *Widows and Their Families*, (Humanities Press, New York)

Mitford, Jessica *The American Way of Death*, (Simon and Schuster, New York) 1963

Worcester, Alfred *The Care of the Aged, the Dying and the Dead*, (Charles C. Thomas, Springfield, Illinois)

2

GUIDES FOR DIFFERENT FUNERALS

While all funerals may follow a usual pattern, appropriate Scripture passages, and expressed thoughts in sermons, hymns and prayers have to be taken into account when it comes to the age, prominence or form of death of the deceased. We thus offer the pastor a few guides in aptness which are ever appreciated by the bereaved.

The Burial of an Aged Person

Because science is lengthening the age span of man, people in civilized countries are living far longer than they did a century or so ago. To reach one hundred years of age is no longer deemed extraordinary. A pastor buries more elderly people than youths. God satisfied them with long life, and at last their frail bark entered port. What a joy it is to visit elderly persons as they near the end, and to find them with "an old age serene and bright," as Wordsworth expresses it, and ready for the journey to the Father's home above. When the end of such a godly person comes, the pastor has no difficulty of expression in committing his body to its resting place. With confidence, the grace of God, exhibited in and through the aged one, can be magnified.

Scriptural Selections

In addition to the recital of Psalm 90, fully quoted earlier, another remarkable portion is the unique portrait Solomon gives us of old age with its attendant infirmities and its victorious end. Although addressed as a warning to youth, it reads —

> Remember now thy Creator in the days of thy youth, while the evil days come not, nor the years draw nigh, when thou shalt say, I have no pleasure in them;
>
> While the sun, or the light, or the moon, or the stars, be not darkened, nor the clouds return after the rain:
>
> In the day when the keepers of the house shall tremble, and the strong men shall bow themselves, and the grinders cease because they are few, and those that look out of the windows be darkened.
>
> And the doors shall be shut in the streets, when the sound of the grinding is low, and he shall rise up at the voice of the bird, and all the daughters of musick shall be brought low;
>
> Also when they shall be afraid of that which is high, and fears shall be in the way, and the almond tree shall flourish, and the grasshopper shall be a burden, and desire shall fail; because man goeth to his long home, and the mourners go about the streets:
>
> Or ever the silver cord be loosed, or the golden bowl be broken, or the pitcher be broken at the fountain, or the wheel broken at the cistern.
>
> Then shall the dust return to the earth as it was: and the spirit shall return unto God who gave it.

Ecclesiastes 12:1-7

* * *

Other fitting Scriptures to choose from at the funeral of an aged person are Psalm 23; Romans 8:35-39; II Corinthians 5:1-10. Knowing that the deceased was a sincere believer the following can be used: Job 19:25-27; Psalm 73:25, 26; I Corinthians 15:55-57; II Timothy 4:7, 8; Revelation 22:4, 5. Themes, based on appropriate texts like the following could be used with profit —

A Good Old Age	Genesis 15:15; 25:8; Isaiah 46:4.
Our Numbered Days	Job 14:5; Psalm 39:4; 90:10, 12.
For an Aged Mother	Psalm 35:14; Proverbs 31:1; Isaiah 66:13.
For an Aged Father	Genesis 25:8; II Kings 2:12.
For a Glad and Glorious Homegoing	Genesis 49:33; Ecclesiastes 12:5; Isaiah 35:10; 51:11; John 14:2; Revelation 21:25.
For Light At Eventide	Proverbs 4:18; Zechariah 14:7; Isaiah 58:8.
A Finished Task	Job 17:11; Ecclesiastes 9:10; John 9:4; 17:4; Hebrews 6:10; Revelation 14:13; 22:12.
Waiting For the End	Job 14:14; Psalm 27:14; II Timothy 4:6, 7.
The Works That Follow	Hebrews 6:10; Revelation 14:13; 22:12; I Corinthians 3:12-15.

Dealing with the span of life, the measure of human existence, and immortality beyond the tomb, the phrase in Psalm 90:10 is most applicable to the death and burial of an elderly person. Another aspect, "Ripe For Harvesting," can be dealt with by taking Job's impressive figure of a long life lived for God:

> "Thou shalt come to thy grave in a full age, like a shock of corn cometh in his season" (5:26).

Although pastors usually gather their tallow from all sources, but make their own sermonic candle, now and again they find themselves hard-pressed for time when an almost ready candle is of great use. Later on, a few gathered funeral sermons are given, but the following outline by J. N. Greene in *The Pastor's Ideal Funeral Book*, is appropriate for the burial of an aged believer. It is based on the psalmist's declaration that "Precious in the sight of the Lord is the death of his saints" (116:15).

Heaven's Estimation of the Death of the Godly

Points and sub-points for the pastor to develop, adding fitting illustrations, sayings and poems are —

1. God's Viewpoint Different From Man's (Isaiah 55:8, 9).
   High and broader — hence God's view of death is different.
   a. Man's view of death
      1. — he sees the loss, broken homes, blighted plans, etc.
      2. — does not see release from sinful world — entrance into glory.
   b. God's view of death
      1. — a sleep (Mark 5:39; John 11:11).
      2. — a blessed change (Revelation 14:13).
      3. — a precious event (Psalm 116:15).

2. Death of the aged, and any saint is precious to God —
   a. Because it is the saint's honorable discharge from warfare
      1. Life is a battle against sin, disease, trial, sorrow.
      2. Life of a Christian is a fight (Romans 7:14-25; Ephesians 6:10-18).
   b. Because it produces transition to a glorified state.
      1. Only the body dies — the spirit is eternal.
   c. Because it results in the saint's exaltation to a satisfied state.
      1. Here — dissatisfaction, mysteries, failures, seeming injustices.
      2. There — perfect understanding, abiding satisfaction (Psalms 16:11; 17:15; 65:4).
   d. Because it represents the saint's welcome home.
      1. Here we are pilgrims and strangers (Hebrews 13:14).
      2. Over there — at home.

3. The Double Message. Warning and Consolation are in the text.
   a. Death is precious for saints only (Daniel 12:2, 3; John 5:29; Hebrews 12:23).

b. Death of ungodly is tragic — eternal darkness and despair.

(Consult the following Chapter on Funeral Sermons)

Suitable Poems

Books of poems by poets with spiritual insight should be at hand for the pastor to select from. Apt verses give an impressive touch to an effective funeral message. Remembering that it is not the length of a life that counts, but the quality of it, the lines of Philip James Bailey can be quoted —

> We live in deeds, not years; in thoughts, not breaths;
> In feelings, not in figures on a dial.
> We should count time by heart-throbs.
>   He most lives
> Who thinks most — feels the noblest — acts the best.
> Life's but a means to an end; that end
> Beginning, mean, and end to all things — God.

W. E. Henley, in *Margaritae Sorori* writes —

> So be my passing!
> My task accomplished and the long day done,
> My wages taken, and in my heart,
> Some late lark singing.
> Let them be gathered to the quiet west,
> The Sundown splendid and serene,
>   Death.

John Greenleaf Whittier taught us to pray —

> Till brief or long, my granted years
> Of life with love to Thee and man;
> Strike when Thou wilt, the hour of rest,
> But let my last days be my best.

As to the glory ahead for those whose days have been long upon the earth, how assuring is the verse Robert Browning gave us —

> Grow old along with me!
> The best is yet to be,
> The last of life, for which the first was made;
> Our times are in His hand
> Who saith: "A whole I planned."
> Youth shows but half;
> Trust God; see all
> Nor be afraid.

Henry Wadsworth Longfellow, the American poet, expresses the end of the ages in this striking way —

> The course of my long life hath reached at last,
>   In fragile bark o'er tempestuous sea,
>   The common harbor, where must rendered be
> Account of all the actions of the past.

Oliver Wendell Holmes, the renowned American author, supplies us with these heart-moving words —

> Build thee more stately mansions, O my soul,
> As the swift seasons roll!
> Leave thy low-vaulted past!
> Let each new temple, nobler than the last,
> Shut thee from heaven with a dome more vast,
> Till thou at length art free,
> Leaving thine outgrown shell by life's unresting sea!
>   (Consult Chapter Four)

Impressive Illustrations and Sayings

Every wide-awake pastor is always looking for illustrative help. He has not only a handy notebook in which to record the captivating poems he reads, but another book in which he makes prisoner all the telling illustrations his reading produces. If illustrations are "the plums in the cake," then sermons, even funeral sermons, will be richer, if apt stories or sayings are used to enforce the message. Herewith are a few pointed ones a pastor can use to enlighten a sermon for the burial of an aged saint. Others can be found in chapter four.

* * *

Sir Winston Churchill, who died in his ninety-first year, when asked on his seventy-fifth birthday whether he had any fear of death, revealed that he was as lighthearted about death as he was of life. His reply was —

> "I am ready to meet my Maker. Whether my Maker is prepared for the great ordeal of meeting me is another matter."

* * *

When he was eighty-five years of age, William E. Gladstone wrote to Lady Dorothy Neville assuring her that he had undreamed of horizons ahead.

> "The year hand of the clock of time is marked eighty-five, and has nearly run its course; I have much cause to be thankful, and still more to be prospective."

* * *

The story is told of a dying saint of ninety-four years who was heard to murmur, "It is too heavy." When asked what was "so heavy" the aged one replied: "Ah! the flesh — the flesh is so heavy. I long to drop it and go."

* * *

A further illustration tells of an aged Christian who, although she had lived many years in an almshouse, manifested great joy when a minister visited her one day. "O Sir, I was just thinking what a change it will be from this poorhouse to heaven!"

* * *

Hugh Macmillan, whose spiritual application of natural objects is well-known, expressed this beautiful sentiment —

> "The day of the death of aged Christians is indeed better than the day of their birth, for rich with all the treasures of spiritual knowledge and experience — the growth and a whole lifetime of discipline — they come to their last hour like the mellow fruit that gathers into itself all the life of a tree, and all the dew and sunshine of the summer, and at last bends and breaks the branch from which it hangs."

* * *

Among pertinent sayings that can be employed we have these gems —

"Heaven's eternal fear is thine" —Dryden.

* * *

"The treasure of everlasting joy" —Shakespeare.

* * *

"We shall be judged not by what we might have done, but what we have been" —Seneca.

* * *

"Give me no guess for the dying pillow" —Joseph Cook.

* * *

"Immortality is the glorious discovery of Christianity" —Channing.

* * *

"The young may die, but the old must!" —Longfellow.

* * *

Fitting Funeral Hymns

Usually, those who have lived long in the service of the Master have their favorite hymn or hymns and the pastor should get to know what they are and use a selection when such saints have been translated to the heavenly choir above. The four favorite hymns of Sir Winston Churchill were —

"The Battle Hymn of the Republic" (Mine eyes have seen the Glory)
"Fight the good fight of faith"
"Who would true valour see"
"O God, our Help in ages past" — all of which were sung by mourners from all over the world at the funeral service in St. Paul's Cathedral, London. To these we can add —

"The sands of time are sinking"
"When my life work is ended"
"How blest the righteous when he dies" — any of which are suitable for the funeral of an aged person who died in the Lord.

One hesitates to suggest a form of prayer for such a particular funeral. The pastor who lives near to the heart of God has

a mind saturated with the promises of God, and likewise a full
knowledge of the life and labors of the aged saint he is burying
and will know how to express himself as he leads the mourners
in prayer. Arthur H. De Long suggests the following supplication for use —

"O Lord God of our fathers, we bless Thee for the holy
triumphs of Thy saints in every age and among all peoples.
We thank Thee for the battles fought, the victories won, and
achievements gained by those who have ceased from their
labors and entered into rest. Thou hast said, 'The hoary
head is a crown of glory, if it be found in the way of
righteousness.' We thank Thee that so often we have been
permitted to see this coronation of goodness in Thy servants.

Bless old people everywhere; some have wandered far in
life's pathway and mayhap have forgotten Thee. Turn, we
pray Thee, their trembling steps into the ways of life.
Prepare all hearts for this great change.

O Lord, we beseech Thee to bless all these relatives and
friends, that in their grief and sorrow at this separation they
may still know Thy goodness and rely on Thy unchanging
love. May the lessons and precepts and holy examples of
Thy servants who have died in the Lord be remembered in
the years to come.

O God, rejoice the souls of Thy servants that none of
those that trust in Thee may be desolate. Make us glad
according to the days wherein we have seen evil. Let Thy
works appear unto Thy servants and Thy glory unto their
children, now and evermore."

Amen!

* * *

A pastor, with an intimate association of an aged member of
his church, would perhaps feel that a prayer like this is too
general, and lacks justifiable personal references. In a public
funeral, he would know what virtues to praise God for in the life
of the one mourned by the relatives and friends present. (See
under Sections Funeral Sermons and Funeral Aids for further
material.)

THE BURIAL OF A MIDDLE-AGED PERSON

Quite naturally, deaths among those who reach middle life are not as numerous as those who reach the allotted span, and often go beyond it. Middle age is described as "being about the middle of the ordinary age of man, between youth and age, variously reckoned to suit the reckoner." The Bible contains some interesting references to those as they reached the noon of life, the old age of which is the sunset. Joshua was forty years old when Moses commissioned him to divide the land of Canaan (14:7), and blessed God for His goodness in keeping him alive for another forty-five years (14:10). Moses was "full forty years old" when he visited the children of Israel (Acts 7:23; Exodus 2:13). The man healed by Peter had reached middle life "above forty years old" (Acts 4:22). The psalmist prayed that he might not be taken away in the midst of his days by the eternal God (102:24). Jeremiah utters a warning that men who live only for earth's possessions may be called by death to leave them — as many have to — in the midst of their days (17:11). Peter divides man's span into two halves, "The rest of his time . . . the time past of our life" (I Peter 4:2, 3).

Sir Walter Scott in *The Lady of the Lake* gives us this descriptive cameo of middle life —

> On his bold visage middle age
> Had slightly press'd its signet sage,
> Yet had not quenched the open truth
> And fiery vehemence of youth.

How different was the sentiment regarding life's meridian in Byron's *Don Juan* — a sentiment reflecting his own experience —

> Of all the barbarous middle ages, that
> Which is most barbarous, is the middle age
> Of man, it is — I really scarce know what;
> But when we hover between fool and sage.

Here is the verse to himself which Byron wrote when he reached his thirty-sixth milestone on his stormy pilgrimage — "On this (January 22, 1824) I complete my thirty-sixth birthday," then followed the pathetic lines —

My days are in the yellow leaf;
The flowers and fruits of love are gone;
The worm, the canker, and the grief
Are mine alone!

This colorful English poet died shortly after, cut off in the midst of his days, a sorrowful and disappointed man. If only Byron's life had been in the hands of Him who died for the world's salvation before He reached His thirty-fourth birthday, Byron might have lived well beyond the sun of life to give the world soul-stirring poems.

In our age there is an increasing number of persons dying as they reach middle life. The stress and strain of business, home problems, heart trouble, diseases, particularly lung cancer brought on by excessive smoking, take their toll of so many who reach the halfway mark. At forty, they become old, and lose the urge and ability to live out a full life. And husbands and wives who die in middle life often leave heavy burdens for others to carry, as pastors know only too well who have to guide and help those thus bereaved. Of course, in the will of God, many who are upright, and noble, God-fearing and full of zeal to serve the Lord through a long life, are called home in the midst of their days. Lazarus of Bethany, although loved of Jesus, was around middle life when he died. Stephen, and several of the apostles were not more than forty to fifty years old when they were martyred for Christ's sake.

Scriptural Selections

Passages already quoted above can be adapted for a funeral service of a person dying in middle life. Other portions that can be read or used as a basis of a sermon are herewith cited —

Sudden Death

As for man, his days are as grass: as a flower of the field, so he flourisheth. For the wind passeth over it, and it is gone; and the place thereof shall know it no more.

Psalm 103:15

Lord, make me to know mine end and the measure of my days, what it is; that I may know how frail I am. Behold, thou hast made my days as an handbreadth; and mine age is as nothing before thee: verily, every man at his best state is altogether vanity. *Psalm 39:4, 5*

* * *

Go to now, ye that say, To day or to morrow we will go into such a city, and continue there a year, and buy and sell, and get gain: Whereas ye know not what shall be on the morrow. For what is your life? It is even a vapour, that appeareth for a little time and then vanisheth away. For that ye ought to say, If the Lord will, we shall live and do this or that. *James 4:13-15*

* * *

Surely every man walketh in a vain shew: surely they are disquieted in vain: he heapeth up riches, and knoweth not who shall gather them. *Psalm 39:6*

* * *

Hear my prayer, O Lord, and give ear unto my cry; hold not thy peace at my tears: for I am a stranger with thee, and a sojourner, as all my fathers were. O spare me, that I may recover strength, before I go hence and be no more. *Psalm 39:12, 13*

* * *

Whatsoever thy hand findeth to do, do it with thy might; for there is no work, nor device, nor knowledge, nor wisdom, in the grave, whither thou goest. *Ecclesiastes 9:10*

* * *

Frailty and Brevity of Life

Man that is born of a woman is of few days, and full of trouble. He cometh forth like a flower, and is cut down: he fleeth also as a shadow, and continueth not. And dost thou open thine eyes upon such an one, and bringest me into judgment with thee? *Job 14:1, 2*

Who can bring a clean thing out of an unclean? Not one. Seeing his days are determined, the number of his months are with thee, thou hast appointed his bounds that he cannot pass: Turn from him, that he may rest, till he shall accomplish, as an hireling, his day.

For there is hope of a tree, if it be cut down, that it will sprout again, and that the tender branch thereof will not cease. Though the root thereof wax old in the earth and the stock thereof die in the ground; Yet through the scent of water it will bud, and bring forth boughs like a plant.

But man dieth, and wasteth away: yea, man giveth up the ghost, and where is he? As the waters fail from the sea, and the flood decayeth and dryeth up: So man lieth down, and riseth not: till the heavens be no more, they shall not awake, nor be raised out of their sleep.

O that thou wouldest hide me in the grave, that thou wouldest keep me secret, until thy wrath be past, that thou wouldest appoint me a set time, and remember me!

If a man die, shall he live again? all the days of my appointed time will I wait, till my change come. Thou shalt call, and I will answer thee: thou wilt have a desire to the work of thine hands. For now thou numberest my steps: dost thou not watch over my sin? My transgression is sealed up in a bag and thou sewest up mine iniquity . . .

The waters wear the stones: thou washeth away the things which grow out of the dust of the earth; and thou destroyeth the hope of man. Thou prevailest forever against him, and he passeth: thou changest his countenance, and sendest him away. *Job 14:4-20*

* * *

Worthlessness of Earthly Things

They that trust in their wealth, and boast themselves in the multitude of their riches: None of them can by any means redeem his brother, nor give to God a ransom for him: (For the redemption of their soul is precious, and it ceaseth forever:) That he should still live forever and not see corruption. For he seeth that wise men die, likewise the fool and the brutish person perish, and leave their wealth to others. Their inward thought is, that their houses shall continue for ever and their dwelling places to all generation; they call their lands after their own names.

Nevertheless man being in honour abideth not: he is like the beasts that perish. This their way is their folly: yet their posterity approve their sayings. Like sheep they are laid in the grave; death shall feed on them; and the upright shall have dominion over them in the morning; and their beauty shall consume in the grave from their dwelling. But God will redeem my soul from the power of the grave: for he shall receive me.

Be not thou afraid when one is made rich, when the glory of his house is increased; For when he dieth he shall carry nothing away: his glory shall not descend after him. Though while he lived he blessed his soul: and men will praise thee, when thou doest well to thyself. He shall go to the genera-tion of his fathers; they shall never see light. Man that is in honour and understandeth not is like the beasts that perish.

Psalm 49:6-20

* * *

From these readings, and other Scriptures, many impressive themes can be developed in sermonic preparation. For instance, a pastor could take —

God the Dispenser of Death	Deuteronomy 32:39; Job 9:12.
Translated in the Midst of Life	Psalm 102:24; Isaiah 38:10; Jere-miah 15:9.
Broken Columns	Job 17:11; James 4:13, 14.
Sun Gone Down at Noon	Jeremiah 15:9; Amos 8:9.
The Rich Young Fool	Psalm 49:6, 7; Matthew 6:19-21; Luke 12:20, 21.
A Little More Time, and a Longer Silver Cord	Job 10:20-22; Psalm 39:11; Ec-clesiastes 12:6; Jeremiah 10:20.

If the middle-aged person was any of the following, then the suggested Scriptures could be applied accordingly —

If a prominent citizen, as well as religious worker	II Samuel 3:38; Psalm 82:7; Luke 12:20; James 4:13, 14.
If conspicuous for godliness	Proverbs 12:2; Acts 7:59, 60.
If a deacon	Acts 6:5; 7:54-64.
If a neighboring pastor	Acts 20:24; II Timothy 4:5.
If a husband	Song of Solomon 3:2; Joel 1:8.
If a wife	Genesis 48:7; Proverbs 31:10-31; Ezekiel 24:18.
If a brother	II Samuel 1:26; John 11:23.
If a sister	Numbers 20:1; Acts 9:36-39.

A most fitting sermon for such an occasion could be preached on the subject, *A Step to Death*, based on two verses namely —

"There is but a step between me and death" I Samuel 20:3.
"Boast not thyself of to morrow; for thou knowest not what a day may bring forth" Proverbs 27:1.

While death is certain and common to all, irrespective of age, none of us knows just when the silver cord will be loosed. Hounded by jealous Saul, David, reaching the meridian of life, felt the nearness of death. There was only a step between him and eternity. Arthur H. De Long gives us these bones to clothe with flesh —

1. *A Step We Must All Take.* (Ecclesiastes 9:5; Hebrews 9:27)
   Science, philosophy, even religion will not prevent it. Law of the Universe (Ecclesiastes 3:19, 20; 8:8).
2. *A Step We Cannot See.* (Ecclesiastes 9:12)
   It may be tomorrow (Luke 12:20; James 4:13, 14). In the midst of life and business. Suddenly, without warning (I Thessalonians 5:2-4).
3. *A Step Of Parting.* (Job 7:9, 10; Ecclesiastes 12:5)
   From world of matter (Job 14:20, 21); from the body (II Corinthians 5:6); from friends, possessions, church, etc.
4. *A Step — Solemn and Mysterious.* (Job 10:21, 22)
   He must be reckless who takes it carelessly.

5. *A Step We Take Alone — Or With Christ.* (Psalm 23:4; Isaiah 43:2; Acts 7:55, 59)
6. *A Step Requiring Necessary Preparation.*
   Sin makes the step dangerous (Romans 6:23; I Corinthians 15:56).
   Sin forgiven brings confidence (Proverbs 14:26, 27; Hebrews 3:6).
7. *A Step Into Heaven, if Christ is the Saviour* (Isaiah 35:10; II Corinthians 5:6, 8)

How true it is, as the poet has reminded us, that —

> Dangers stand thick through all the ground,
>   To push us to the tomb;
> And fierce diseases wait around
>   To hurry mortals Home.

(Consult next chapter on Funeral Sermons)

Suitable Poems

Here, again, the pastor will consult "the poets' corner" in his library for apt lyrics to enforce his message. The favorite poem of Abraham Lincoln, who himself was assassinated when he was only fifty-six years of age, was that from the pen of William Knox —

> Oh why should the spirit of mortal be proud?
> Life a fast-flitting meteor, a fast-flying cloud,
> A flash of the lightning, a break of the wave,
> He passes from life to his rest in the grave.
>
> 'Tis the wink of an eye, 'tis the draught of a breath,
> From the blossom of health to the paleness of death.
> From the gilded saloon to the bier and the shroud —
> Oh why should the spirit of mortal be proud?

Homer, the traditional Greek epic poet of the eighth century, is credited with these lines from the *Iliad* —

> Like leaves on a tree the race of man is found,
> Now green in youth, now withering on the ground:
> Another race the following spring supplies:
> They fall successive, and successive rise.
> So generations in their course decay,
> So flourish these when those have passed away.

J. G. Whittier's poem of great consolation is most apt —

> I know not what the future hath,
> Of marvel or surprise;
> Assured alone that life and death
> His mercy underlies.
>
> And so beside the silent sea
> I wait the muffled oar,
> No harm from Him can come to me
> On ocean or on shore.

How essential it is to set our house in order so that no matter when our last enemy comes, ours will be the necessary preparation for the continuation of life in a sunnier clime.

> Death comes with reckless footstep
> To the hall and hut:
> Think you that Death will tarry, knocking
> Where the door is shut?

Impressive Illustrations and Sayings

From history, and his own experience, a pastor can gather many windows to let more light into his funeral sermon. Perhaps one of the most appealing illustrations to use at the type of funeral we are presently considering is that of Sir Winston Churchill's radio tribute to King George VI, when on February 6, 1952, a grief-stricken nation learned of his death. Because of the abdication of his brother, the Duke of Windsor had greatness thrust upon him. Like Abraham Lincoln, the beloved monarch died just past middle age at the age of fifty-six. In his moving reference Churchill said —

> "During these last months the king walked with death, as if death were a companion, an acquaintance whom he recognized and did not fear. In the end death came as a friend, and after a happy day of sunshine and sport, and after a 'good night' to those who loved him best, he fell asleep, as every man who strives to fear God and nothing else in the world may do."

King George's great-grandfather, Prince Albert, Queen Victoria's husband, who died at forty-two years of age, left this testimony just before his death —

"I have had wealth, rank and power. But if this were all I had, how wretched I should be now!

> Rock of Ages cleft for me,
> Let me hide myself in Thee."

* * *

Robert Ingersoll, the famous American agnostic and orator, had a younger brother to whom he was deeply attached and who died just as he reached his fortieth year. At his funeral, Robert Ingersoll in his oration gave utterance to a most hopeless farewell. He was not able to speak of a glorious reunion in eternity. He said:

"The lovely and loving brother, husband, father and friend died where manhood's morning almost touches noon, and while the shadows still were falling toward the west. He had not passed on life's highway the stone that marks its highest point; but, being weary for a moment, he laid down by the wayside and, using his burden for a pillow, fell into that dreamless sleep that kisses down his eyelids still. While yet in love with life and raptured with the world, he passed to silence and pathetic dust.

Yet, after all, it may be best — just in the happiest, sunniest hour of all the voyage, while eager winds are kissing every sail, to dash against the unseen rock, and in an instant hear the billows roar above a sunken ship. For whether in mid sea or 'mong the breakers of a farther shore, a wreck must mark at last the end of each and all.' "

* * *

How different from this forlorn peroration was the triumphant testimony of Paul who could say that death was not the end, but gain: and that to depart and be with Christ was far better! *Talk as we like, plead as we may, death without God is terrible.* We are thrice blessed if we have learned that —

> "This, only this, subdues the fear of death —
> A pardon bought with blood! with blood Divine."

For further striking descriptions of death, which the pastor can forcibly apply, his attention is directed to our later chapter on funeral aids.

As to a fitting prayer, it should contain references to the frailty and uncertainty of human life, and the terrible reality of death; to the solemn responsibilities of preparedness for the unexpected; to the unfailing love and compassion of God; to the bereaved of the one removed in the noon of life. At the graveside, a committal prayer should express a final reminder that there is only a step between any of us and death.

O Lord, it is so true that in the midst of life we are in death. We brought nothing into this world, and it is certain we can carry nothing out, but our character. The Lord gave and the Lord hath taken away; blessed be the name of the Lord. We now commit the mortal remains of this friend to the earth from which the body came — earth to earth, ashes to ashes in the sure and certain hope of resurrection. The grace of the Lord Jesus Christ, the love of God, the fellowship of the Holy Spirit be with all of us who remain. Amen!

Funeral Hymns

If a printed form of service is prepared for the funeral service and the hymns to be sung are set forth in full, from the following selection two or three more or less relevant to the particular age of the deceased might be used.

"Crossing the bar" —Tennyson
"Forever with the Lord" —Montgomery
"Friend after friend departs" —Montgomery
"Jesus, Lover of my soul" —Charles Wesley
"Fade, fade each earthly joy" —Bonar
"Rock of Ages cleft for me" —Toplady

THE BURIAL OF A YOUNG PERSON

The Bible carries many attractive stories as well as solemn warning for young hearts. In these modern times when the accent is upon youth, and industry sometimes acts as if a person is too old at forty for heavy responsibilities, many youth problems would be solved if only the young would believe that the favor of God is promised to those who, in life's fair morning secure "the pearl of truth." John Drinkwater wrote of —

> Age with all the best of all his seasons done
> Youth with his face towards the upland hill.

Youth lays the foundation of noble manhood or womanhood when its face is toward the holy hill of God. Scripture portions to follow remind us that young people die, as well as others who no longer retain the dew of youth. It is for this reason that one of the wisest of men exhorted the young to remember God (Ecclesiastes 12:1). The world never despises youth when Christ is chosen as the center and circumference of life.

Longfellow gave us a most expressive verse on the nobility of youth lived to the full for the highest in life —

> How beautiful is youth! how bright it gleams
> With illusions, aspirations and dreams!
> Book of beginnings, story without end,
> Each maid a heroine, and each man a friend!

The death of a young person as he or she reaches the portal of opportunity and independence, is always a sore grief to parents who have surrounded their children with so much affection and godly influence. All that was willingly sacrificed to give them a good education so that they could take their place in the world seems wasted, and the question arises, "Why were they not allowed to live and fulfill their purpose?" With our finite minds we cannot penetrate the inscrutable wisdom of God, but faith can be ours to rest in the fact that because of His perfection He cannot make a mistake. "What I do, thou knowest not, but thou shalt know hereafter" (John 13:7).

> Why what we long for most of all
> Eludes so oft our eager hand,
> Why hopes are crushed, and castles fall —
> Up there, some time we'll understand.

Placetus, the ancient philosopher, would have us know that, "He whom the gods love dies young, whilst he is full of health, perception and judgment." Our loving heavenly Father loves all the young, whether they recognize Him as their gracious Father through Christ, or no; and sometimes calls home those who have "the morn and liquid dew of youth," as Shakespeare puts it, because of His loving purpose to use them in heaven.

Scriptural Selections

Such is the wonder of the Word that no matter what duty a pastor has to perform he can find all necessary help in its sacred pages. It is indeed a poignant hour when he has to conduct the funeral of a bright, gifted, much-loved, Christian young person whose flower of youth has been blasted by death. He can string together these pearls of truth —

Remember now thy Creator in the days of thy youth, while the evil days come not, nor the years draw nigh, when thou shalt say, I have no pleasure in them. *Ecclesiastes 12:1*

* * *

As for man, his days are as grass: as a flower of the field, so he flourisheth. For the wind passeth over it, and it is gone, and the place thereof shall know it no more.

Psalm 103:15

* * *

In the morning sow thy seed, and in the evening withhold not thy hand: for thou knowest not whether shall prosper, either this or that, or whether they both shall be alike good . . . Therefore remove sorrow from thy heart, and put away evil from thy flesh: for childhood and youth are vanity.

Ecclesiastes 11:6, 10

* * *

Nevertheless I will remember my covenant with thee in the days of thy youth, and I will establish unto thee an everlasting covenant. *Ezekiel 16:60*

* * *

My days are swifter than a post: they flee away, they see no good. They are passed away as the swift ships: as the eagle that hasteth to the prey. *Job 9:25, 26*

* * *

Teach us to number our days, that we may apply our hearts unto wisdom . . . Let thy work appear unto thy servants, and thy glory unto their children. *Psalm 90:12, 16*

* * *

If the funeral is that of a young man the following portions could be read —

In the morning sow thy seed, and in the evening withhold not thine hand: for thou knowest not whether shall prosper, either this or that, or whether they both shall be alike good.

Truly the light is sweet, and a pleasant thing it is for the eyes to behold the sun: But if a man live many years, and rejoice in them all; yet let him remember the days of darkness; for they shall be many. All that cometh is vanity.

Rejoice, O young man, in thy youth; and let thy heart cheer thee in the days of thy youth, and walk in the ways of thine heart, and in the sight of thine eyes: but know thou, that for all these things God will bring thee into judgment. Therefore remove sorrow from thy heart, and put away evil from thy flesh; for childhood and youth are vanity.

Ecclesiastes 11:6-10

* * *

Man that is born of a woman is of few days, and full of trouble. He cometh forth like a flower, and is cut down: he fleeth also as a shadow, and continueth not. *Job 14:1, 2*

* * *

For all flesh is as grass, and all the glory of man as the flower of grass. The grass withereth, and the flower thereof falleth away. *I Peter 1:24*

* * *

And it came to pass the day after, that he went into a city called Nain; and many of his disciples went with him, and much people. Now when he came nigh to the gate of the city, behold, there was a dead man carried out, the only son of his mother, and she was a widow: and much people of the city was with her. And when the Lord saw her, he had compassion on her, and said unto her, Weep not. And he came and touched the bier: and they that bare him stood still. And he said, Young man, I say unto thee, Arise. And he that was dead sat up, and began to speak. And he delivered him to his mother.   *Luke 7:11-15*

* * *

Jesus said unto her, I am the resurrection, and the life: he that believeth in me, though he were dead, yet shall he live: And whosoever liveth and believeth in me shall never die.

John 11:25, 26

* * *

If the funeral is of a young woman, then these Scriptures could be used —

Then shall the kingdom of heaven be likened unto ten virgins, which took their lamps, and went forth to meet the bridegroom. And five of them were wise, and five were foolish. They that were foolish took their lamps and took no oil with them: But the wise took oil in their vessels with their lamps. While the bridegroom tarried, they all slumbered and slept. And at midnight there was a cry made, Behold, the bridegroom cometh; go ye out to meet him. Then all those virgins arose, and trimmed their lamps. And the foolish said unto the wise, Give us of your oil; for our lamps are gone out. But the wise answered, Not so; lest there be not enough for us and you: but go ye rather to them that sell, and buy for yourselves. And while they went to buy, the bridegroom came; and they that were ready went in with him to the marriage; and the door was shut. Afterward came also the other virgins saying, Lord, Lord, open to us. But he answered and said, Verily, I say unto you, I know you not. Watch therefore, for ye know neither the day nor the hour wherein the Son of man cometh. *Matthew 25:1-13*

* * *

Peace I leave with you, my peace I give unto you: not as the world giveth, give I unto you. Let not your heart be troubled, neither let it be afraid.   *John 14:27*

* * *

As the pastor prayerfully meditates upon a message suitable for the burial of a young person, he might be able to develop one of the following suggestive titles —

For the Death of a Son	Genesis 22:16; II Samuel 18:33; Jeremiah 6:26; 9:21; 48:17; Isaiah 40:30; Luke 7:12.
For the Death of a Daughter Taken in the Flower of Age	Judges 11:40; Mark 5:35. I Samuel 2:33; Job 14:2; Psalm 127:3-5.
Broken Plans	Job 17:11; James 4:13, 14.
The Creator and Guide of Youth	Psalm 90:14; 110:3; Proverbs 2:17; Ecclesiastes 12:1; Isaiah 26:19; Jeremiah 3:4.
Polished Stones for the Temple	Psalm 144:12; I Kings 7:22; Revelation 7:13-15.

In addition to the foregoing seeds for sermons, it may prove helpful to outline a message or two. If, for instance, the young person being buried is a male, the occasion could be used to impress young men present among the mourners to be ready to meet the king of terrors when he comes.

Preparation for the Life Beyond

Text: Matthew 24:44. Reading Matthew 24:32-51.

Thoughts to expand — While life and death are symbolized by seedtime and harvest yet are they different. Nature is unvarying in her seasons, not so death which comes at any time at any age. Seems unnatural for one young, strong life full of promise to be taken.

Time of event is unknown — any day or hour. God veils

our eyes. He knows the moment, we don't. Uncertainty commands readiness. Preparedness increases pleasure. Godliness profitable for life here, as well as hereafter. Psalm 90:14; Ecclesiastes 11:9. How can a young man be ready? Repentance toward God and faith in Christ (John 3:3, 14-16). Assurance of sins forgiven (Revelation 21:27). Delight in doing divine will (Matthew 24:42-51; 25:31-46).

For the burial of a young woman, if the pastor has knowledge of her previous Christian life and character, he might take *The Sleep of Death*, with the basic verse "The damsel is not dead, but sleepeth" (Mark 5:39), and the narrative as the Scripture portion.

> But when the sun in all his state
>   Illumined the eastern skies,
> She passed through Glory's morning gate,
>   And walked in Paradise.
>
> — Aldrich

Dealing with the simile of sleep, attention could be drawn to its contrasts and comparisons in our Lord's chosen term of "sleep" to "describe" death (John 11:11-14), and also in the references in the epistles (Acts 7:60; I Corinthians 15:6, 51; I Thessalonians 4:13; II Peter 3:4). Then emphasis could be given to the fact that both revelation and reason proclaim the likeness between sleep and death in these particulars —

Both render the subject unconscious to human conditions of time and space.

Both are assuredly followed by awakened life.

Both have their national rational place in the subject and make him more than he could be without them.

Both render the subject unconscious to experiences deemed so essential to life and bring him again to the fullest fellowship of life as though they had not been interrupted.

Care must be taken to show that sleep, when applied to death, refers only to the body, not the soul. The dust sleeps in the earth awaiting resurrection, but the soul of the Christian is as conscious the hour after death as the hour before it. The believer, the moment the body dies, goes to be with the Lord, and is alive for evermore (see Luke 16:19-31). How apt is the phrase Shelley gave us, "How wonderful is Death, Death and his brother Sleep!"

(See Funeral Sermons)

Suitable Poems

From Tennyson's long, remarkable poem, *In Memoriam*, written in memory of a young friend who had died, there are several verses which the preacher could adapt in his funeral message at the burial of a young person —

"Death has made
His darkness beautiful with thee."

From Longfellow there are two or three different verses that can likewise be used —

O, what hadst thou to do with cruel death
Who was so full of life, or death with thee,
That thou shouldest die before thou hadst
grown old?

* * *

Then fell upon the house a sudden gloom,
A shadow on those features fair and thin;
And softly from that hushed and darkened room
Two angels issued, where but one went in.

That the young who die in the Lord are as "flowers in deathless bloom" was also in the mind of Richter, the German author when he wrote —

"The youth of the soul is everlasting, and Eternity is youth."

Shakespeare touched upon the mystery of the ravages of cruel death among lives so fresh and full of promise in his *Romeo and Juliet* —

Death lies on her, like an untimely frost
Upon the sweetest flower of all the field

* * *

Death, that hath sucked the honey of their breath,
Hath had no power yet upon thy beauty;
Thou art not conquered. Beauty's ensign yet
Is crimson in thy lips, and in thy cheeks,
And death's pale flag is not advanced there.

The poem of Edgar Allen Poe, the American writer and poet is incomparable, especially for the funeral of a virtuous young woman —

Come, let the burial rite be read,
The funeral song be sung!
An anthem for the queenliest dead
That ever died so young —
A dirge for her the doubly dead
In that she died so young.

Impressive Illustrations and Sayings

As so many of the brave martyrs and covenanters died for Christ in "life's fair morning," striking illustrations can be gathered from their records of how they met the command of sergeant death! Instances of this can be found in our section devoted to "Famous Last Sayings." All the warriors who died young, and whose light was intense while it lasted, "fulfilled a long time in a short time." One crowded hour of the glorious life is worth an age of ineffectual years.

Robert Murray McCheyne, the saintly minister of Dundee, Scotland, died before his twenty-fifth birthday, and the whole nation mourned the passing of one who accomplished so much in such a short life. Once he wrote in his diary, "O God, give me grace so to live that when dead I shall be missed." And how greatly missed he was! Through his saintliness of character, love for the souls of men, and Spirit-inspired preaching he drew Scotland nearer God, and the nation still misses the impact of his impassioned ministry. The godless, reckless way that many young people live today makes it evident that the world will not miss them if death should lay its hold upon them.

When Isaac Watts wrote his renowned Calvary hymn, "When I survey the wondrous Cross," the second line read —

"Upon which the *young* Prince of Glory died."

Our Lord had not long left the youth stage behind when He suffered and died upon the tree. He was a few months beyond His thirty-third year of young manhood when He cried in triumph, "It is finished!" He did not come to the end of His earthly sojourn an old, decrepit man. As the poet beautifully expressed it, Christ was —

> Dead ere His prime
> Not one golden hair was grey,
> On His crucifixion day

He had great possessions in the past eternity, but unlike the rich young ruler, He sold all that He had in order to come and die for the salvation of a poor lost world. How the young are missed when death claims them if they have lived at the utmost for the highest!

The story is told of a young captain in the British forces who found after a battle, that his Bible had been struck by a bullet, which penetrated to the verse, "Rejoice, O young man, in thy youth . . . But know for all these things God will bring thee into judgment" (Ecclesiastes 11:9). The Bible saved his life, and impressed by this miracle, it became the means of saving his soul.

How sadly youth errs when it deems the Christian faith something which the old, when they come to die, should think about! They fail to realize that they themselves, although young, strong and free, are in the midst of death; that their breath is only in their nostrils and may be withdrawn at any moment; and that it is incumbent upon them to be devoted to "the young Prince of Glory," so that when death does come it will find them ready to enter the land where eternal youthfulness will be theirs.

> Dust, to its narrow house beneath!
> Soul, to its place on high!
> They that have seen thy look in Death
> No more may fear to die.

In the funeral prayer, the pastor will give utterance to human helplessness in the presence of death, especially when the young are smitten by its power. Expression will be given to God's fatherly tenderness, and how His infinite wisdom is the answer to all our troubled questionings. There will be a reference to the Saviour who at an early age finished His God-given task, and to the sentiment that it is not the length of life that counts but the quality of it. Comfort for a saddened home and sorrowing parents in the house of death will be prayed for, and the hope expressed that the passing of the young son — or daughter — as they were blossoming into life, will be sanctified unto all who remain. Such a prayer will close with the plea that other young lives in contact with the one mourned for, will be brought to a full submission to the claims of Christ, and thus be united in glory with the friend taken from earth at the noon of life.

As a brief committal prayer at the cemetery, the following could be used —

> O Father of mankind, as we rest all that is mortal of our young friend in this silent green acre, we sorrow not as others who have no hope, for our trust is in Him who said, "I am the resurrection and the life: he that believeth in me, though he were dead, yet shall he live: and whosoever liveth and believeth in me shall never die." Knowing, therefore, that the one whose body we are committing to the earth was Thine, we believe that he, too, is alive forevermore. Thus we commit his ashes to ashes, his dust to dust in the sure hope of a glorious resurrection through the Saviour our young friend dearly loved. May grace be ours to live as unto Thee until the day breaks and the shadows flee away. Amen!

Funeral Hymns

In the section of almost all denominational and general hymn-books devoted to "Hymns for the Young," appropriate hymns can be found for use at a funeral service of a young person. For instance, we have —

"Not now but in the coming years"
"Go thou in life's fair morning, go in the bloom of youth."
"How can we forget Him, our blessed Redeemer?"
"Jesus is our Shepherd, wiping every tear."
"Just as I am without one plea."
"Jesus Saviour, pilot me."

THE BURIAL OF A CHILD

Death itself, no matter at what age it may come to us, or how it is brought about, is ever a mystery. This is why we stand in silence in the death chamber or at a grave. Yet somehow we never think of it as a mystery when the aged die. When the allotted span of life is reached and passed, death is expected. The old have encountered the storms of life, and the Pilot comes to guide them to the haven of eternal rest. But our feelings are different when the youngest are cut down. We expect the full-bloom flower to wither and die, but are disappointed when a bud of promise is nipped by a blasting frost. Why does God permit cradles to be emptied, and loving hearts to be robbed of their treasure? The answer is beyond our present understanding. "Now we see through a glass darkly." Perhaps, when we reach heaven we shall discover that had some children been allowed to live they might have entered a life of sin and crime, but that God in His wisdom removed the little flowers to His garden before they were destroyed by the evils of this world. Further, many a parent has come to understand that there is a worse experience than that of having a baby in heaven.

Are these not thoughts that must possess a pastor's mind as he visits homes where the most distressing and long lasting of all griefs is that of the death of a child prayed for, eagerly desired, gratefully received, yet snatched away by death ere it has hardly commenced to live? The grief is more poignant if the child is the only one. Such a shattering blow is hard to recover from. The death of an infant or very young child may not have the same emotional upset, if there are other children or every possibility of other children being born in the home. "Blessed be childhood," says an ancient writer, "which brings down something of heaven into the midst of our rough earthliness." Alas, all too frequently such a breath of heaven vanishes all too soon! How expressive are the lines of the poet, Alonzo Rice! —

> How brief the stay, as beautiful as fleeting,
> The time that baby came with us to dwell;
> Just long enough to give a happy greeting,
> Just long enough to bid us all farewell.

Death travels down the thickly settled highway,
At shining marks they say he loves to aim;
How did he find, far down our lonely byway
Our little one who died without a name?

Scriptural Selections

A loving-hearted pastor, especially if he is a parent, and has lost a dear child of his own, finds the burial of a little one a somewhat distressing occasion if young parents are so distraught over the death of the baby they yearned for. The pastor's memory will be active, yet grace will be his to make the mourners' shares of the comfort he himself experienced if his had been the sorrow of a tiny grave. Wonderful, is it not, that the Bible offers so many words of consolation for the pastor to choose from at such a sorrowful time?

* * *

The Comforting Words of Jesus

And they brought young children to him, that he should touch them: and his disciples rebuked those that brought them. But when Jesus saw it, he was much displeased, and said unto them, Suffer the little children to come unto me, and forbid them not: for of such is the kingdom of God. Verily I say unto you, whosoever shall not receive the kingdom of God as a little child, he shall not enter therein. And he took them up in his arms, put his hands upon them, and blessed them.

Mark 10:13-16

* * *

At the same time came the disciples unto Jesus, saying, Who is the greatest in the kingdom of heaven? And Jesus called a little child unto him, and set him in the midst of them, And said, Verily I say unto you, Except ye be converted, and become as little children, ye shall not enter into the kingdom of heaven. Whosoever therefore shall humble himself as this little child, the same is greatest in the kingdom of heaven, And whoso shall receive one such little child in my name receiveth me. But whoso shall offend one of these little ones which believe in me, it were better for him that a millstone were hanged about his neck, and that he were drowned in the depth of the sea.   *Matthew 18:1-6*

* * *

Take heed that ye despise not one of these little ones; for I say unto you, That in heaven their angels do always behold the face of my Father which is in heaven.

Even so it is not the will of your Father which is in heaven, that one of these little ones should perish.

Matthew 18:10, 14

* * *

The Voice of Weeping

A voice was heard in Ramah, lamentation, and bitter weeping; Rachel weeping for her children refused to be comforted for her children, because they were not. Thus saith the Lord; Refrain thy voice from weeping, and thine eyes from tears: for thy work shall be rewarded, saith the Lord; and they shall come again from the land of the enemy. And there is hope in thine end, saith the Lord, that thy children shall come again to their own border.   *Jeremiah 31:15-17*

If I be bereaved of my children I am bereaved.

Genesis 43:14

* * *

The Lord gave, and the Lord hath taken away; blessed be the name of the Lord.   *Job 1:21*

* * *

And I saw a new heaven and a new earth; for the first heaven and the first earth were passed away; and there was no more sea. And I John saw the holy city, new Jerusalem, coming down from God out of heaven, prepared as a bride adorned for her husband. And I heard a great voice out of heaven, saying, Behold, the tabernacle of God is with men, and he will dwell with them, and they shall be his people, and God himself shall be with them, and be their God. And

God shall wipe away all tears from their eyes; and there shall be no more death, neither sorrow, nor crying, neither shall there be any more pain: for the former things are passed away. *Revelation 21:1-4*

* * *

And he showed me a pure river of water of life, clear as crystal, proceeding out of the throne of God and of the Lamb. In the midst of the street of it, and on either side of the river, was there the tree of life, which bare twelve manner of fruits, and yielded her fruit every month: and the leaves of the tree were for the healing of the nations.

And there shall be no night there: and they need no candle, neither light of the sun; for the Lord God giveth them light: and they shall reign for ever and ever. *Revelation 22:1, 2, 5*

* * *

The Resignation of Faith

David therefore besought God for the child; and David fasted, and went in, and lay all night upon the earth. And the elders of his house arose, and went to him, to raise him up from the earth; but he would not, neither did he eat bread with them. And it came to pass on the seventh day, that the child died. And the servants of David feared to tell him that the child was dead: for they said, Behold, while the child was yet alive, we spake unto him, and he would not hearken unto our voice: how will he then vex himself, if we tell him that the child is dead? But when David saw that his servants whispered, David perceived that the child was dead: therefore David said unto his servants, Is the child dead? And they said, He is dead.

Then David arose from the earth, and washed and anointed himself, and changed his apparel, and came into the house of the Lord and worshipped: then he came to his own house; and when he required, they set bread before him and he did eat. Then said his servants unto him, What thing is this that thou hast done? Thou didst fast and weep for the child, while it was alive; but when the child was dead, thou didst rise and eat bread. And he said, While the child was yet alive, I fasted and wept: for I said, Who can tell whether God will be gracious to me, that the child may live? But now he is dead, wherefore should I fast? can I bring him back again? I shall go to him, but he shall not return to me.   *II Samuel 12:16-23*

* * *

Blessed be God, even the Father of our Lord Jesus Christ, the Father of mercies, and the God of all comfort; Who comforteth us in all our tribulation, that we may be able to comfort them which are in any trouble, by the comfort wherewith we ourselves are comforted of God.

II Corinthians 1:3, 4

* * *

The many references to children in the Bible afford the pastor much material to draw upon. We have —

The death of the first-born of Egyptians (Exodus 12:29, 30).
The death of David's child by Bathsheba (II Samuel 12:14-23).
The death of Jeroboam's child (I Kings 14:13).
The death of the widow's child (I Kings 17:17).
The death of the Shunamite's child (II Kings 4:19, 20).
The death of the innocent babies (Matthew 2:16-18).
The death of the child of Jairus (Matthew 9:18-24).

A study of various passages provides one with many themes to use for the comfort and encouragement of those who are rendered childless or who lose a child.

The Child Is Well	II Kings 4:18-26; Job 1:21; Mark 7:37.
The Children's Chorus in Heaven	Psalm 8:2; Matthew 18:10; 21:15, 16; Revelation 14:1-5.
The Fragrance of Dead Flowers	I Samuel 2:33; Song of Solomon 6:2; I Peter 1:24; I Corinthians 15:20.

The Children As Jewels	Malachi 3:17; Matthew 18:10; Mark 10:14; Zechariah 8:5.
The Encircling Arms	Isaiah 40:11; Matthew 18:14; Mark 10:16.
The Children Around the Throne	Zechariah 8:5; II Samuel 12:23; Revelation 22:4.

Isaiah reminds us that the death of a child desolates the home, the heart, and future plans, yet makes heaven nearer and dearer (Isaiah 49:21, See Matthew 6:21).

Jeremiah describes how disconsolate a mother is when she weeps for the child who is not. Such inconsolable grief is natural and comes to many (Jeremiah 31:15-17; Mark 5:38, 39). But such weeping is only for a night. Joy cometh in the morning (II Samuel 12:23; Psalm 30:5).

Solomon portrays our beloved Lord as a Gardener coming down into His garden to gather lilies (Song of Solomon 6:2). And what a striking comparison there is between lilies and little ones. Both are pure, delicate and beautiful; yet easily sullied and soon faded. The heavenly Beloved knows best when He transplants His lilies to heaven before their beauty fades.

Perhaps the most telling sermon a pastor could preach at the funeral of a child is one based on David's belief in immortality when, learning of the death of his newborn, baby boy, he said —

"I shall go to him, but he shall not return to me"

(II Samuel 12:23).

Excessive grief had been David's while the child's life was in the balance, but once dead, the king knew that his grief could not bring back the baby. So, resigning himself to the will of God, David was consoled to know that heaven held a treasure for him.

Occasionally inquiring hearts, resigned to the divine will in the removal of a young child, seek the pastor's views as to various aspects of children in heaven. It is to be hoped that the sentiments herewith expressed will be of service when certain questions arise. First of all, it must be made clear that there is no more brutal and false doctrine ever concocted than that which asserts that unbaptized children go to perdition. Such monstrous teaching is absolutely contrary to the character of God and opposed to the evangel of Christ. Augustine taught that all children dying unbaptized in the Roman Church would be damned. Something of this blasphemous and ghastly teaching can be found in a volume for children by a Roman Catholic priest, the Rev. Father Furniss, bearing the title, *The Light of Hell*. Think of this horrible paragraph —

> "Little child, if you go to Hell there will be a devil at your side to strike you. He will go on striking you for every minute for ever and ever without stopping. The first stroke will make your body as bad as the body of Job. The second stroke will make your body twice as bad as the body of Job. The third stroke will make your body three times as bad as the body of Job. The fourth stroke will make your body four times as bad as the body of Job. How, then, will your body be after the devil has been striking it every moment for a hundred million years without stopping?"

All that we can say is that any man who could write such terrible and senseless words was of the devil himself. How destitute of compassion he must have been, and how different his attitude from that of the Master who said of the children, "Of such is the kingdom of heaven"! Bless God, there are no babies and children under the age of responsibility in hell!

Dying before they reached the years of moral choice and the power to discern between right and wrong, they passed right into the presence of Jesus in virtue of His atoning work upon the cross. Original sin they did have, but that was covered by the blood. Practiced sin they did not have and therefore were not guilty of transgressions incurring the wrath of God. As for the mentally deficient, if born insane, they enter heaven upon the same conditions.

How came those children there,
Singing, Glory, Glory, Glory?

* * *

> Because the Saviour shed His blood
> To wash away their sin,
> Bathed in that precious purple flood,
> Behold them white and clean,
> Singing, Glory, Glory, Glory.

A matter perplexing the heart of many a Christian mother who has a baby in heaven, is whether that little one will remain in the same state above. Do girls and boys have their purpose in heaven as such? A twin answer is offered for this question. First, there are those who feel that without children in heaven much would be missed by the godly parents who bore them; that as we depart — whether child, youth or patriarch — so we remain; that when the body is raised at Christ's Return, He will raise it as it was but withal glorified. Thus a child of one year will still be, in size and appearance, a child a year old; that a mother will have her child as a *child* forever. Preaching on the theme of recognition in heaven, Bishop Simpson of America broke out in his sermon with the question: "What would heaven be to me without my Wilbur?" — Wilbur being his dear son, whom death had recently claimed.

The second approach is that growth and increase will be characteristic of children in heaven; that the mother crossing the threshold of the life beyond will instantly discover that her child, or children, have grown to a glorified maturity. Under the creative touch of God, and under the tutelage of their angel-teacher, they steadily grew into a perfect character. F. C. Spurr tells of a friend of his who had lost a child, and who sent him a silver printed card bearing the words —

> "In memory of our little Donald, lent to us for two years; the sunshine of our home, recalled by the Father, now at school with the angels for his tutors."

Such a hope is a comforting and satisfying one for those who believe that the lambs gathered to His bosom reach the full stature of glorified manhood or womanhood. Just what the exact future holds for the children who die before their innocency is blasted by the sins of this life, Scripture does not say. In this faith, however, we can rest, that our dear ones are not lost to us, and that no matter what change may overtake them, they will still be ours; and that all the redeemed, like the angels, will possess endless youth, activity, power, knowledge and holiness; and experience the same immortal happiness, dignity and divine favor; be lovely, beautiful and glorious in the sight of God.

> My knowledge of that life is small,
>   The eye of faith is dim;
> But 'tis enough that Christ knows all,
>   And I shall be with Him.

An error that must be corrected is that children, or for that matter, all the saints, are to be angels in heaven. That hymns are not always Biblical is evident from this children's hymn, a verse of which reads —

> I want to be an angel
>   And with the angels stand;
> A crown upon my forehead,
>   And harp within my hand.

The same mistake is found in the lines —

> Too thick in every graveyard
>   The little hillocks lie,
> But every hillock represents
>   An angel in the sky.

Our Lord clearly taught that we are to resemble the holy angels in some of their attributes, but never that we are to be angels. All the saints in heaven will be glorified human beings, as distinct from the angels, as they are distinct from the Lord of Glory. Neither are we to spend eternity "singing around the throne" with harp in hand. Song there will be, but also service fitted to our individuality. As real beings, possessed of spiritual bodies and quickened intellects, we shall be active, serving the Lord as we cannot here below because of the trammeling influences of the flesh.

Suitable Poems and Hymns

One of the most tender and consoling poems ever written for bereaved parents was that by Charles Wesley, so appropriate for the funeral service of a young child.

Wherefore should I make my moan,
    Now the darling child is dead?
He to rest is early gone,
    He to Paradise is fled.
I shall go to him, but he
Never shall return to me.

God forbids his longer stay,
    God recalls His precious loan.
He hath taken him away
    From my bosom to His own.
Surely what He wills is best;
Happy in His will I rest.

Faith cries out, "It is the Lord,"
    Let Him do what seems Him good.
Be Thy holy name adored,
    Take the gift a while bestowed.
Take the child no longer mine,
Thine he is, forever Thine.

If, as Byron reminds us, "Heaven gives its favorites early death,"
then we appreciate these further fitting verses by Longfellow —

There is no flock, however watched and tended,
    But one dead lamb is there!
There is no fireside, howsoe'er defended,
    But has one vacant chair.

The air is full of farewells for the dying
    And mournings for the dear.
The heart of Rachel, for her children crying,
    Will not be comforted.

As one of the favorite interpretations of the death of a dear
child is that of the Lord coming as a Gardener to gather His
beautiful flowers, we can understand the feeling of the gardener
who asked, in anger, when he saw the broken stem of a rare and
choice flower upon which he had bestowed loving care, "Who
plucked my flower?" The master replied, "It was I," and the
disappointed gardener held his peace. It must have been this
thought which Lord Lytton had in mind when he wrote his
poem *There Is No Death! The Stars Go Down*, the last verse of
which reads —

He leaves our hearts all desolate;
    He plucks our fairest, sweetest flowers;
Transplanted into bliss, they now
    Adorn immortal bowers.

Longfellow likewise dwells on the same simile of babies as flowers in his heart-moving poem, *The Reaper and the Flowers*, the last lines of which are —

> O, not in cruelty, not in wrath,
>   The reaper came that day;
>   'Twas an angel visited this green earth
>   And took the flowers away.

Among the many hymns for children that can be adapted to a funeral service of a church, choice can be made from the following —

> "We need love's tender lessons taught."
> "Wherefore shall I make my moan."
> "Little children, little children."
> "There's a Friend for little children."
> "When He cometh, when He cometh."
> "Saviour, who Thy flock art feeding."

Impressive Illustrations and Sayings

Although the tender slender thread may be suddenly broken, and the shuttle cease to fly, the design is being completed elsewhere, for God's purpose is always fulfilled. Such has been the comforting hope of many God-fearing parents whose little ones God took to people heaven. Thomas Boston experienced that a little child's death is often a bitter and poignant blessing. God's sword, like Cid's sword, wounds that it may heal: that a crown of thorns can be transmuted into a crown of gold. "To bury his name was indeed harder than to bury his body," Boston murmured when he laid his infant Ebenezer to sleep. But there is no burying such a name, for Boston knew that his dear little Ebenezer was in heaven, beckoning and alluring him to the heights above.

How moving is the description Charles Dickens gives us of little Nell!

"She was dead. There upon her little bed she lay at rest. The solemn stillness was no marvel now. She was dead — no sleep so calm, so free from trace of pain, so fair to look upon. She seemed a creature fresh from the hand of God and waiting for the breath of life, not one who had lived and suffered death. Dear, gentle, patient, noble Nell was dead."

That God often overrules in such a grief and sanctifies the sorrow, using it for His beneficent ends is proven in the experience of Josephine Butler (1828-1906), who became the friend and representative of tarnished girlhood, as the result of the tragic death of her little daughter, Eva. With her minister husband, Josephine Butler had been on a vacation in Europe, leaving their little one at home. How excited the child was when the night of her parents' return came! Hearing the sound of carriage wheels outside and commotion in the hall of the home, little Eva sprang from her bed, dashed out of her room and jumped on the banister rail to see "Daddy" and "Mummy" again. But the tot lost her balance and fell with a thud on the floor below. Let the shocked mother herself relate the incident —

> "Never can I lose that memory — the fall, the sudden cry and then the silence. It was pitiful to see her helpless in her father's arms, her little drooping head resting on his shoulder, and her beautiful golden hair all stained with blood falling over his arm."

But the sudden death of that dear lamb was to mean life for many lost sheep, for the distracted mother could find no comfort until she dried her tears and devoted herself to the salvation of wayward and motherless girls in the grim outside. Thus her sorrow was not lost, but sanctified and used by God in a mighty way.

Many a pastor has found that a funeral prayer at the burial of a precious child is a difficult task. He yet learned, however, that the gracious Comforter came to his aid and led him to pray feelingly. One cannot improve on the prayer, which Arthur De Long suggests —

> Our Father of love, of great compassion and of tender mercy, we come to Thee at this time, not because of any concern for the soul of this dear child lying here in the dreamless sleep of death — for it is eternally safe with Thee — but we come to Thee for these, thy servants, whose hearts

are broken with the consciousness of their grief and loss. Do Thou behold their sorrow and desolation, and help Thou them in this their time of need.

Forgive us if, in the hour of our darkness, we have for one moment doubted either Thy wisdom or Thy love. We know that Thou art too wise to make mistakes and too good to be unkind. May we see light in Thy light.

We could give Thee thanks for this little life, which has called forth so many ministrations of love, service and sacrifice, and bound us to it with cords of tenderest affection. Let us not forget its sweet lessons of love, innocence and purity. May this little messenger of God have accomplished its mission to all hearts.

Grant that these bereaved ones may be soothed and comforted today, and that their lives may be sweetened and softened by this loss, and give to them the grace of submission to Thy will and wisdom, and an increased devotion to Thee and to Thy service. And let us comfort our hearts with the hope that if these little ones can not return to us, we may go to them. All we ask is for Jesus' sake. *Amen*

To the brief committal prayer, one might use the following —

Our Father in heaven, whose love is unfailing and whose wisdom is infinite, Thou hast taken back to Thyself the sweet and innocent child whose dust we commit to the earth in the sure and certain hope of a glorious resurrection through Jesus Christ our Lord. Grant to the sorrowing parents and relatives, "beauty for ashes, the oil of joy for mourning, and the garment of praise for heaviness." *Amen!*

The Burial of an Unknown Person

All who are engaged in pastoral work know what it is to be asked to bury someone unconnected with any church. If a pastor is well-known in a community because of his far-reaching pulpit or radio ministry, he is the first to be called upon to conduct a funeral for those who have no religious affiliation whatever. Relatives of the deceased know of the pastor as a good man, and ever willing to assist those in need, thus his help is sought. Such funerals can eat up valuable time. Still, eager to extend the cause of Christ, such opportunities of bringing the Gospel to bear upon the irreligious, are fitted into a busy schedule, with the prayer that the mourners will be made to realize the need of being ready to meet God in eternity.

The conduct of the funeral of one completely unknown to the pastor, however, is no easy matter. All he can do is to follow a general order of service, having hymns expressing the necessity of preparation for the life beyond, and the Bible call to repentance toward God and faith in Jesus Christ. His prayer, too, will voice the uncertainty of life, the blessed assurance of those who are saved by grace, and the comfort of the bereaved. In his funeral sermon, the pastor, with a passion for souls, will preach, not *at* the people but *to* them of the provision God has made for all who embrace His salvation. Guided by the Spirit, the pastor can grasp the occasion and make it to impress upon all who are present the reality of eternal things. Many a pastor has had the joy of welcoming into his church, relatives of the unknown deceased all because of his willingness to come to their aid in a time of grief.

The Burial of a Suicide

Whether people die naturally, or are killed or end their own life, they have to be buried, and in the main, burials presuppose the offices of a minister of religion. The rapid rise of suicides in our time is a matter of deep concern to all who have the welfare of human society at heart. Back in the seventeenth century Edward Young wrote of Britain as being "infamous for suicides." Such a description is truer of the country today, also of America, for the latter had over 21,000 suicides last year, and the former, 7,000. Shakespeare reminds us that the Everlasting One "fixed His canon against self-slaughter." The law calls a suicide, "a criminal upon himself."

Alas, through the stress and strain of our neurotic age those guilty of self-murder are on the increase, with the most common form of suicide being that of an overdose of drugs, or sleeping pills! Reverses in business, frustrated ambitions, marital problems, and physical and mental strain, drive people to end it all.

Suicide seems to be a refuge for despair. But a person killing himself or herself does not end his trouble by taking his own life. John Churton Collins of the eighteenth century wrote that, "Suicide is the worst form of murder, because it leaves no opportunity of repentance." Think of the horror, and worse, grief which the ungodly suicide finds in the caverns of the doomed, as Judas did after he had hanged himself!

If a pastor has to conduct the funeral of the suicide, and the suicide is one of his congregation, his task is by no means light. Sometimes a Christian, suffering intense pain, becomes mentally deranged and takes a way out of such personal anguish. While suicide can never be condoned, extenuating circumstances must be sympathetically considered. For the funeral of such a person a Psalm like the forty-second, with its call to forsake despair, could be read, as well as Psalm 107, with its hope for those who are at wit's end corner. In his message, the pastor, if cognizant of all the factors responsible for the self-destruction of the deceased, should extol the virtues and witness manifested when the person was normal, and proclaim the love of our compassionate God who ever remembers our dust-frame. As for the funeral prayer, it should commence by magnifying God for His mercy and for His perfect knowledge of the trials and testings of His children, and then go on to express the power of faith to keep them sane and safe in the hour of dire need. Intercession will be made for understanding and sympathetic hearts, seeing we do not know how we would act if brought to the same trials as the deceased. Our only hope is that we might prove the sufficiency of His grace, and thus live out our days, until He Himself severs the silver cord.

Hymns at such a service should be chosen from those fragrant with God's eternal thought of us, such as, "O Love that wilt not let me go," or "O troubled heart there is a balm" and others eloquent with the truth of relief from all our pain and problems as we enter heaven, like, "Forever with the Lord" or "Peace! perfect peace! in this dark world of sin."

At the cemetery, the committal prayer should be of a general nature.

The Burial of a Member of the Armed Forces

In these days of "wars and rumours of wars," this type of funeral is all too common. Because of the rapid spread of communism with its utter disregard of human rights, the upsurge of nationalism, and the lust for power on the part of would-be dictators, solemn pacts and treaties are spurned and war ensues. It is thus that peace-loving nations like Britain and America find themselves embroiled in bloody conflicts to establish justice and liberty, as in Viet Nam and Aden. Often those who fall in battle find graves in foreign soil, but there are others whose remains are flown home for burial in their own community. Sometimes men in the forces are killed accidentally in their own home base, or old pensioners die in hospital or in their own homes, and a military funeral is arranged. As large crowds usually gather for such an occasion, the local pastor or chaplain is confronted with a unique opportunity of witnessing to the reality of eternal truths.

Scriptural Selections, Messages, Poems, Illustrations

As the Bible abounds in wars, the exploits of fighting men, and military metaphors, it is not difficult to seek out appropriate passages to read at the funeral of one who served his country. For instance, the minister could read with effect —

> The sacrifice and courage of David's men to secure water (I Chronicles 11:15-19).
> The war from which there is no discharge (Proverbs 21:1; Ecclesiastes 8:8).
> Fighting the good fight of faith (II Timothy 4:7, 8; Philippians 3:14; Hebrews 12:1).
> The last battle of soldiers and sailors (Joshua 23:14; Psalms 55:8; 107:29, 30; Revelation 20:13).
> God's warriors and their warfare (Ephesians 6:10-18).

Paul's portrayal of a good soldier (II Timothy 2:1-4) provides the preacher with sufficient matter for a telling sermon. Serving one's country implies submission, discipline, obedience, distinction of uniform, the willingness to suffer and die — which aspects can be stressed in the lives of those who follow the divine Captain and serve beneath His flag (Psalms 20:5; 60:4; Song of Solomon 2:4; 6:4, 10).

Of poems that could be woven into the texture of the message, the preacher could use *The Conqueror's Grave*, by Bryant, and *Dirge For A Soldier*, by G. H. Boker. From the hymn books, lyrics with a martial air can be gathered.

> "Fight the good fight with all thy might."
> "Onward, Christian Soldiers."
> "Jesus, Saviour, pilot me" (if funeral is of a sailor).
> "Crossing the Bar."
> "Am I a soldier of the Cross?"
> "There's a royal banner given for display."
> "Stand up, stand up, for Jesus"
> "Christian seek not yet repose."

Illustrative material can be gathered from the biographies of military and naval heroes. There was Nelson who, as he died at the Battle of Trafalgar, breathed out his creed: "God and my country." Severely wounded he still commanded his men saying: "England expects every man to do his duty." Sir Henry Havelock was the renowned British general whose heroic stand at Lucknow shines in the annals of the British Army. As he died of disease, he confessed, "For more than forty years I have so ruled my life, that when death came, I should meet it without fear." General Charles Gordon was another who served God and his country. At the Fall of Khartoum, his head was severed from his body and placed on a pole for all to see. Being a godly man, he was not afraid to die, and was never ashamed of his Master. When on active service, Gordon's subordinates knew that when a white handkerchief was outside his tent, that he was at prayer. This was his signal that he was in the presence of the divine King and must not be interrupted. Edith Louisa Cavell was the brave British nurse who died before a firing squad during the First World War, and whose memorial is not far from that of Nelson's at Trafalgar Square, London. As she came to die, her dying affirmation had been: "This I would say, standing as I do in view of God and His eternity: I realize that patriotism is not enough. I must have no hatred or bitterness toward anyone." She needed more than love of her country to sustain her in such a grim hour, and as a pronounced Christian she knew that the everlasting arms were around her.

There is a further well-known incident the preacher can use as he urges the mourners to be ready when the roll is called up yonder. After a terrible battle a young soldier lay in the field hospital mortally wounded. All was silent, but suddenly the dying soldier called "Here!" A surgeon hastened to his side and asked what he wanted. "Nothing," said the soldier, "they were calling the roll in heaven, and I was answering to my name." Immediately after, he was gone to join the white-robed army above.

In his funeral prayer, the pastor, apart from commending the sorrowful relatives to the Lord, will refer to the Christian influence of the deceased among his comrades, if there is the knowledge that he was a believer, and color his intercession with the use of military symbols found in the Bible and in the hymns used.

At the graveside, before the bugle call is sounded, if it is a military funeral, a short committal prayer like the following can be uttered —

> "O, Thou, who art the Captain of salvation, made perfect through Thy sufferings, we bless Thee for the march of another soldier which is over. His battles are over, and his last victory won. We therefore commit his remains to the grave under the arching sky to await the bugle call of the resurrection. Earth to earth, dust to dust, until the Lord appears in glory. Amen!"

* * *

For a burial at sea, thoughts from "Crossing the Bar" — "For those in peril on the sea" — "Jesus, Saviour, pilot me" could be used with effect, and a portion like Revelation 20:11-15 with its reference to the sea giving up its dead, would be applicable as the corpse was committed to the deep.

> Good Pilot of the awful main,
> Let us not plead Thy love in vain;

Jesus, draw near with kindly aid,
Say, "It is I; be not afraid!"
 Keep by Thy mighty hand, oh keep
 The dwellers on the homeless deep.

The Burial of a Distinguished Person in City or Nation

There are occasions when pastors have to conduct the funeral of those who, although they were devoted members of the church, were yet conspicuous in communal, national or international affairs. Such a funeral always draws mourners from all walks of life. The most impressive funeral of this kind was that of Sir Winston Churchill which brought to St. Paul's Cathedral one of the greatest assemblies of kings and queens, rulers and presidents, and representatives of all walks of life ever witnessed. On a far lesser scale, a pastor sometimes has to bury one of outstanding fame, in his own community, and because of the unusual crowd gathered for such a funeral, he has a wider opportunity of witness for the Master.

Scripture portions and themes relative to such a funeral could be taken from these suggested ones —

A Prince Has Fallen	II Samuel 3:38; Psalm 82:7.
Treasure in Earthen Vessels	II Corinthians 4:7-14, 16, 17.
Differing Stars in Glory	I Corinthians 15:35-58; Daniel 12:3; Matthew 13:43.
The Frailty of Life	Psalms 39:4, 5; 103:15-17.
Heaven's Illustrious Roll	Matthew 11:1-11; Mark 9:33-37.
Final Assize of the Great and Small	Revelation 20:11-15; 21:1-7.

While the funeral sermon must contain references to the deceased's accomplishments in civic, national or philanthropic realms, care must be taken not to gild the lily. If, in spite of his achievements and acquirements, he was a sincere and humble follower of the Lord Jesus, then emphasis must be given to the fact that the basis of his greatness was his Christian faith and moral worth; and that being diligent he secured fame and fortune and now stands before the King of kings. Philip Bailey's memorable lines can be enlarged on with great effect —

> We live in deeds, not years; in thoughts, not breaths;
> In feelings, not in figures on a dial.
> We should count time by heart-throbs. He most lives
> Who thinks most — feels noblest — acts the best.

* * *

The poem of Horatius Bonar, Scottish Presbyterian preacher and poet could also be adopted —

> He liveth long who liveth well!
>   All other life is short and vain;
> He liveth longest who can tell
>   Of living most for heavenly gain.
>
> He liveth long who liveth well!
>   All else is being thrown away;
> He liveth longest, who can tell
>   Of true things truly done each day.

* * *

There are many historical illustrations the pastor can draw from to enforce the thought that the greatness of many sprang from a heart experience of the grace of God. We have Lord George Lyttleton, who died in 1773, who received fame as a British statesman, and who, in public life was not ashamed to own the Master. Influenced by William Law's *Serious Call*, of which Lyttleton said that it was "one of the finest books that ever was written," he left this testimony behind —

> "The evidence of Christianity, studied with attention, made me a firm believer of the Christian religion. I have erred and sinned, but have repented."

Thomas Jefferson said of George Washington, father and first president of his country, as he heard of the great man's death —

> "His integrity was most pure: his justice the most flexible I have ever known — no motives of interest or consanguinity, of friendship or hatred, being able to bias his decision. He was in every sense of the word, a wise, a good and a great man."

Toward his end Washington said to his physician: "Doctor, I have been dying a long time, my breath cannot last long — but I am not afraid to die."

* * *

Thomas Arnold was prominent not only as the gifted and famous Headmaster of Rugby School, England, but also renowned as a preacher and author. Because he was intensely religious, his manifest scholarship held a subordinate place to his lofty estimate of duty toward God and those he taught at the school that gave its name to a popular sport seeing it was conceived at *Rugby*. It has been said of Arnold that his was "a regal supremacy of the moral and the spiritual element over his whole being and powers."

* * *

William Wilberforce, who was the champion of the abolition of Negro slavery, was another whose religion was at the heart of his outstanding statesmanship and his philanthropic works. He was a most pronounced evangelical and warmly supported all efforts to reach the privileged as well as the underprivileged with the Gospel of Christ. One of his sons said of his last days that, "he seemed like a person in the actual enjoyment of heaven within."

The pastor's prayer at the funeral of a distinguished person, apart from its element of supplication for the comfort of bereaved relatives, will be shaped by a meditation upon the Scriptures we have suggested. The prayer should also express a plea that while the mourners may never be able to reach the deceased's renown and achievement they can equal him in the Christian traits of his character.

The committal prayer at the graveside should be after this order—

"O most merciful Father, how true it is that death knows no distinctions. The great and small fall beneath his scythe. As we commit the remains of this honored servant of Thine to their resting place, may grace be ours whether our days be many or few, or life, known or unknown, ever to be at our best for Thee. Grant us Thy peace on our onward way. Amen!"

As for suitable hymns, if the deceased had any favorite ones, these should be included. If an independent selection has to be made then the necessary number might be chosen from the following well-known compositions —

"Abide with me, fast falls the eventide."
"O God our help in ages past."
"Jerusalem the Golden."
"Ye servants of the Lord, each in his office wait."
"There is a land of pure delight."

THE BURIAL OF A COMPANY SUDDENLY KILLED

There are times when disaster strikes and many homes in a community are shadowed by grief. An airplane explodes or crashes, a train is wrecked, miners in a pit are crushed or choked to death, earthquakes and volcanos destroy lives and property and tornados and hurricanes lash towns claiming a fearful toll of human life. If the bodies are terribly mangled, they are sometimes buried in a common grave. It sometimes happens that several of the dead are members of one church, and widespread sorrow prevails. Ancient Egypt became a nation with drawn blinds when the final death-plague occurred, and there was not one house in which there were no dead (Exodus 12:30; Jeremiah 9:21). What a tragedy it is if a local church has to bury several of its members at the same time!

During the last century violent deaths have increased in a manner uaparalleled in human history. Casualties on the roads claim thousands of lives *daily*. When death is a sudden and unexpected event, "a bolt from the blue," hearts are stunned by such a swift call and find it more difficult psychologically, to adjust themselves to such a shock. As *Clinical Theology* expresses it in the Syllabus on "Bereavement, Grief and Mourning" —

"The sudden death shatters the normally continuing sense of personal orientation and reality, and of contact with the external world of persons and things. The mind is bewildered and behavior shows it. Activity may be aimless and little more than a restless turning from task to task. Bewilderment may be accompanied by a strange loss of the customary feelings of reality about faith and the external world. The tree is riven to its roots again."

In such circumstances, the pastor will need great wisdom and tenderness of approach as he seeks to establish confidence in God's wise and loving providence. Through the sudden and surprising removal of a dear one, deep attachments are swiftly severed and may result in a certain hostility toward God on the part of those overwhelmed by unexpected loss.

How solemn and unenviable is the responsibility of the pastor in such terrible circumstances! What can he say when death has come to so many, so suddenly? What approach can he make to doubts arising in some hearts as to the love and wisdom of God? Unless the roots of his own faith are deep in God's unerring justice and mercy, he will not find a covert from the storm of grief that has engulfed many hearts.

It is wonderful to know that in the Bible there are precious portions applicable to any catastrophe that can overtake man. Paul speaks of "the comfort of the Scriptures" (Romans 15:4), and these enable a pastor to speak comfortably to people so distressed. Passages he will ponder over before the burial of those tragically killed will be those speaking of God's inscrutable providences (Psalm 97:2; John 13:7), and yet of His unfailing comfort and relief (Isaiah 51:12; II Corinthians 1:3, 4). For reading at the burial, Psalm 90 and I Corinthians 13 are incomparable. For a funeral sermon at such a time what more appropriate verse could be taken as the basis than the one Paul gives us in his "hymn of love."

> Now we see through a glass, darkly:
> But then face to face (I Corinthians 13:12).

Over against the mysteries of life we must place the paradise of revelation. Emphasis will be given to the fact that our finite minds cannot fully understand the actions of our infinite God. We are unable to see God's plans in their completeness. We may only see a block of marble, but the sculptor can see in it an angel to release. Is this not the sentiment Robert Browning embodied in the lines? —

> Let us leave God alone!
> Why should I doubt He will explain in time
> What I feel now, but fail to find the words.

When darkness descends because of the anguish and desolation of unexpected bereavement, and there seems to be no solution to the sorrowful enigmas of life, we must think of Him who cried, "My God, my God, why hast thou forsaken me?" Paul did not live in the gloomy "now," but counterbalanced it with a glorious "then," and Paradise alone will bring us the why and wherefore of human tragedy.

> God knows the way, He holds the key,
>   He guides us with unerring hand;
> Sometime with tearless eyes we'll see;
>   Yes, there, up there, we'll understand.

Grief-gripped in Gethsemane, Jesus could yet pray, "Nevertheless not my will but thine be done" (Luke 22:42). Thus, as one writer expresses it —

> "Calamity
> Is man's true touchstone."

Expressions after this manner by the preacher will assure the mourners whose hearts are numbed with sorrow over sudden desolation that —

> The Hand that holds the ocean's depth can hold my small affairs,
> The Hand that guides the universe can carry all my cares.
> I'm glad I cannot shape my way, I'd rather trust His skill;
> I'm glad the ordering is not mine, I'd rather have Thy will.
> I do not know the future, and I wouldn't if I might,
> For faith to me is better far than faulty human sight.

As for the funeral prayer, it should create the atmosphere of peaceful resignation to the divine will that cannot err, and reassure troubled hearts that there is a joy, seeking us through pain. Interceding for the bereaved, the pastor will ask that all patience may be granted to those who weep and mourn until in heaven above they read the meaning of their tears, and then praise "the Hand that guided and the Heart that planned." If the company suddenly killed, are buried together, a brief committal prayer such as this could be offered —

> "O merciful Father, behind whose frowning providence there is a smiling face, Thou knowest our frame, and understandest our grief and perplexity over this great calamity. Assure our hearts anew that Thou art able to cause even the most sorrowful experiences to work together for good. We commit these precious bodies, dust to dust, ashes to ashes, confident of the resurrection of the dead. Amen!"

MESSAGE FOR A MEMORIAL SERVICE

In the course of their ministerial duties, pastors are often called upon to participate in national Memorial Days. America has a Memorial Day or Decoration Day, kept on May 30th in honor of those who were killed in the U. S. Civil War of 1861-1865, and observed as a legal holiday. Then there is Remembrance Day or Veterans' Day, observed on November 11th, held in honor and commemoration of those who died in the two world wars. In London, England, there is always the elaborate ceremony at "The Cenotaph." But in all cities and towns religious and civic and military representatives meet in the city's center, or in a cemetery where some of the fighting forces are buried, for a remembrance service of a more or less religious nature. Usually on such occasions, the valor and sacrifice of those who died in the struggle for liberty are extolled.

These Remembrance Days are not for the purpose of glamorizing war, which never loses the hellish significance which General Sherman gave it, but to pause and think of the shedding of blood in the preservation of the country from tyranny and oppression. Recalling the sacrifice of so many soldiers, sailors and airmen, we praise God for the privilege of living in a land where we have the liberty to worship God as He directs, and to vote and speak according to the dictates of conscience. How apt and impressive is Rudyard Kipling's *Recessional* for such a time of remembrance —

God of our fathers, known of old,
   Lord of our far-flung battle-line,
Beneath whose awful Hand we hold
   Dominion over palm and pine —
Lord God of Hosts, be with us yet,
Lest we forget — lest we forget!

The tumult and the shouting dies;
   The Captains and the Kings depart;
Still stands Thine ancient sacrifice,
   A humble and a contrite heart.
Lord God of Hosts, be with us yet,
Lest we forget — lest we forget!

Far called, our navies melt away,
   On dune and headland sinks the fire;
Lo, all our pomp of yesterday
   Is one with Nineveh and Tyre!
Judge of the Nations, spare us yet.
Lest we forget — lest we forget!

If, drunk with sight of power, we loose
   Wild tongues that have not Thee in awe,
Such boastings as the Gentiles use.
   Or lesser breeds without the Law.
Lord God of Hosts, be with us yet,
Lest we forget — lest we forget!

For heathen heart that puts her trust
   In reeking tube and iron shard,
All valiant dust that builds on dust,
   And guarding, calls not Thee to guard,
For frantic boast and foolish word,
Thy mercy on Thy people, Lord! Amen

If a Memorial or Remembrance Day falls on a Sunday, or recognition of same is made on a Sunday, the pastor can combine such an event with the permanent "memorial day" when Christians partake of the "memorial" or "remembrance feast" — the Lord's Supper. At a Communion service, the hearts of all present are reminded of the necessity of another sacrifice that must ever be kept in memory, namely, the supreme sacrifice of Him who died at Calvary for our spiritual emancipation from Satan and sin.

By Christ redeemed, in Christ restored,
We keep the memory adored,
And show the death of our dear Lord
   Until He come.

In unforgettable sentences the Master urged us to remember His dying love. "This do in remembrance of me" (Luke 22:19). "The Holy Ghost . . . shall . . . bring all things to your remembrance" (John 14:26). The combination of these two sentences in our Lord's teaching indicates the two sides of the remembrance involved in the memorial or sacramental feast He Himself instituted. There is the human side — "This do," and this command is fulfilled when we come together in obedience to the express will of the Master. Knowing the weakness of memory, He urges us to sit at His table as often as we can to remember His dying love. Then there is the *divine side* — "The Holy Spirit shall bring to your remembrance." Happily we are not left to our own effort to stimulate remembrance. It is the function of the Spirit to quicken our memories and take us back to the cross. We are sluggish, forgetful, and need to be reminded constantly by One who witnessed the great tragedy of Calvary. Thus the wind of Pentecost keeps alive the fire of Calvary. The Holy Spirit keeps the cross before our eyes, and He delights to carry our minds back to the victory of Calvary that made possible His descent at Pentecost.

As we gather round the table of the Lord, the Spirit constantly reminds us of three realms of truth and quickens our faith in such: *God* in His love, justice and holiness is presented; *Christ* in His sacrifice and humiliation is proclaimed; *Man* in his sin, need and impotence is manifested. And how we should praise the Spirit for His goodness in stirring up our minds by way of remembrance.

If an annual Memorial, or Remembrance Day should fall on a Sunday, and a Pastor uses the occasion to coincide with the "remembrance feast," perhaps the following outline might serve to provide him with thoughts for the message at the table.

Dr. J. R. Miller, in one of his incomparable devotional volumes, tells the story of a dear mother who lost her only child. What grief was hers! Now and again she went to the drawer and, taking out the toys, shoes and garments of her departed baby, would fondly handle them. Such articles inspired remembrance and remembrance in turn produced many qualities.

1. *Remembrance Quickens Love*

The love of that mother for her child was quickened or intensified by remembrance. That mother did not bury her love in a grave. Love is of God and therefore it is eternal. Love will last as long as God. It is thus that the Holy Spirit seeks to stimulate a purer, deeper love for Jesus. He takes us back to the cross where we seem to hear the Saviour ask — "Lovest thou Me?" And as we remember the cost of our salvation, what reply have we, but, "I love Thee for wearing the thorns on Thy brow." We hear a good deal about a passion for souls, but our tragedy is that we have not enough passion for Jesus Himself. Count Zinzendorf's confession was, "I have but one passion, and that is He." Do we love Him, seeing that He first loved us?

One difference, however, between the fond mother Dr. Miller writes about and ourselves is this — she had seen the face of her child, and looked into his eyes, and kissed his cheeks, hugging him to her breast. But we have never seen the face of Christ. Our eyes have never seen that radiant form of His. The Holy Spirit, however, makes Him real to faith. Whom having not seen, we love (I Peter 1:8; John 20:29).

> Yea, though I have not seen and still
> Must rest in faith above,
> I love Thee, dearest Lord, and will
> Unseen but not unknown.

2. *Remembrance Begets Gratitude*

As that lonely-hearted mother handled her baby's possessions, gratitude would rise to God for the life given, even though his stay was so short. She would be grateful that her child died young and innocent, being spared the sin and shame of life. Gathered home to God's pure lilies, the mother would come to know that after all, there are worse experiences than that of having a child in heaven.

Does not the Spirit work in the same way? He makes real the debt of gratitude we owe. The purpose of the table each time we sit to eat and drink is that we might say with deeper feeling, "Thank You, Lord, for bearing my curse and dying for me." Why, Christ Himself gave thanks as He broke the bread, which He said would symbolize His broken body. Gave thanks? What did *He* say "thank you" for? Was it not for the assurance that by His death a mighty deliverance would be wrought for multitudes?

3. *Remembrance Fosters Holiness*

Thinking her dear child in heaven, made holy forever, faith would enable the mother to whom we have referred, to visualize her loved one, dressed in white forever. And such contemplation would inspire her to face life with a more earnest endeavor to live a life corresponding in some measure to the purity of her child above.

A great question troubling many hearts is whether our departed loved ones are cognizant of what goes on below; whether they can see and know all things of human interest. Well, if they share the omniscience of the Lord into whose likeness they have been transformed, then they do not sorrow as those of earth, for, like their Lord, they too can see the end from the beginning.

While, of course, our holy dead can have no contact with us, yet is it not a spur to holy living to realise that kindred spirits are not very far away, and that possibly they maintain a definite interest in our lives? This, we know, the remembrance of the crucified, risen and exalted yet absent Lord leads us to a more complete surrender. As we remember that His grief and pains were involved in our redemption, what else can we do but be holy and have lives surrendered to Him?

There may be some uncertainty regarding the knowledge of earth our departed have, or of how near they are to us, but of this we are certain, Jesus is ever near. We feel and know that He is at hand. And the more conscious we are of His presence, the deeper our consciousness of sin, and the more determined our desire to live as unto Him.

> I see Thee not, I hear Thee not,
>   Yet Thou art oft with me;
> And earth has ne'er so dear a spot
>   As when I meet with Thee.

4. *Remembrance Inspires Anticipation*

Let us turn again to the fond mother we have been considering. The house is quiet and memory is active. Going to the drawer yet once again, she handles those precious shoes and little garments, and sits and thinks of the love she bore and still bears the innocent child. How grateful she is to God for the joy of motherhood, even though it was short-lived. Rising from her reveries, she goes on her journey inspired to holier living, realizing that the separation is but for a little. E'er long she will clasp him again, and death will never more tear him from her heart! With half of her heart in heaven she brushes aside her tears and is cheered by the thought of a blissful reunion.

Is this not the way the Holy Spirit works? In His effort to quicken our remembrance He bids us look back to the grave where Jesus lay — up to His present abode — forward to the day when we shall see Him face to face. As the mother is saved from nursing her grief by remembering the future and gathers hope thereby, so the Holy Spirit inspires anticipation. As we take the bread and the wine in our hands, He reminds us that such remembrance is only "till He comes." Atonement and advent are seen to be two halves of one whole. And what a gathering of the ransomed that will be! "And with the morn, those angel faces smile." His face, however, will be the One all the redeemed will adore. The mother went out to meet her beloved child, to be joined with him forever, but Christ is coming to meet us. And what a blessed meeting that will be! And such blessed anticipation as well as love, gratitude and holiness, is fostered by the remembrance feast.

Dr. J. R. Miller also tells the story of a young man who went abroad, but before setting out was presented with a watch having upon its dial miniatures of his loved parents. "Take this watch," said his father, "and carry it with you in all your journeyings. Every time you look to see the hour, the eyes of your loving father and mother will look into yours. When you see these home faces, remember that we are thinking of you and praying for you. Go to no place where you would not want us to see you. Do nothing you would not want us to see." In the Lord's Supper,

Jesus has given us His own picture, so to speak. His broken body and shed blood are ever before us as we participate. And as we look at the dial bearing His portrait, we are saved from doubt, fear and sin. Remembrance intensified by the Spirit leads us to greater nobleness and beauty of life. And, living in the light of His return, we have the assurance that when He summons us we shall pass out to meet our Beloved without the blush of shame, and memory will give way to everlasting praise as we see His face.

SUPPLEMENTARY READINGS

De Long, Arthur H. *Pastor's Ideal Funeral Book*, (Abingdon, Nashville) 1910

Greene, J. N. *The Pastor's Ideal Funeral Book*

Lee, Mark W. *The Minister and His Ministry*, (Zondervan, Grand Rapids) 1960

3

SELECTED FUNERAL SERMONS

The importance of having the right approach in a funeral message is stressed by Dr. John Broadus in his monumental work on homiletics — *The Preparation and Delivery of Sermons*. In the section dealing with sermons for particular occasions Dr. Broadus quotes from Kidder's homiletics —

> A prevailing fault of funeral discourses is the occupation of too much time with generalities or truths that have no special application to the existing circumstances. It is far better to confine such discourses to narrower limits, and to that particular range of thought which all will recognize as to the pertinent.

Although a church full of mourners presents a pastor with a golden opportunity of giving them a fleeting glimpse, he should never take advantage of such an event. The trend is for a short message rather than a more elaborate and formal discourse. One has read of an undertaker who informed a friend, "When the family have no church affiliation, we always recommend a certain cleric because he gives us an exact 12-minute address for everybody, so we can push through three funerals an hour in the same chapel." But whether the sermon is brief or otherwise, the true pastor will have need of God's grace to seize the time to recommend the Gospel of consolation, to impress the need of personal holiness on the part of believers present, and to call those who are not Christ's to prepare to meet God.

As hearts are sorrowful and softened at such a time, the funeral

sermon should clearly indicate the way of eternal life. Because
of the prevalence of sorrow and death, the pastor is called to
minister the comfort of the Gospel. As John M. English expresses
it in his volume, *The Minister and His Ministry* —

> "Every true pastor is a *paraclete* in the function of en-
> couraging and strengthening by consolation, and the longer
> he remains in a community the exercise of this function of
> his ministry greatly increases. He is surrounded by trouble
> of every sort, and people look to him as they look to no
> other for comfort. This phase of his work makes expensive
> draughts upon his vitality — physical, mental and spiritual;
> but it is a price to be paid in the prosecution of his divine
> calling. It takes the very life out of him, but for this he has
> given his life. A ministry of sympathy he cannot escape,
> and should not wish to escape, and he must have a sym-
> pathy to minister and a sympathy in ministering."

While some reference to the departed is in order if he or she
was a loyal member of the church, the pastor must remember that
he is not a mere eulogist of the dead. What he does say should
uplift the mourners and inspire them to emulate the noble witness
of the one mourned. Dr. Broadus wisely warns that what is said
of the deceased "must be *scrupulously true,* though not neces-
sarily *all* the truth, for this would be superfluous and sometimes
painful." Exaggerated praises should be shunned. To quote
again —

> "When the departed was a Christian, he should speak
> chiefly of that fact, bringing out anything in the character
> or course of the life which he knows, and others will recog-
> nize, to be worthy of imitation. When the departed was not
> a Christian, he may sometimes lawfully speak a few soothing
> words as to anything which specially endeared the de-
> ceased to his friends. But this must be done, if done at all,
> without exaggeration and it is a solemn duty to avoid saying
> one word which suggests that these good points of character
> afford any ground of hope for eternity."

If the deceased made no profession of faith, but was commend-
able in character and not afraid to die, the pastor must not err

by suggesting that although he was not a Christian as generally understood, his soul can be left to the mercy of God. Where there was no evidence whatever of a life lived in Christ, nothing whatever should be said about the deceased's eternal future. To raise false hopes is surely sinful. If the deceased was known to be wicked, the pastor in real kindness will say nothing about him, but preach a message on the certainty of eternity, and the necessity of being ready to face God.

To guide the preacher as to an appropriate message for a funeral we herewith include a few specimens gathered from various sources. In *Patterns for Preaching*, Harry C. Mark gives us these skeletons —

Death Conquered
Text: Hebrews 2:14, 15

1. Our Lord shared humanity with us.
2. Our Lord became human that He might die.
3. Our Lord died in order that He might conquer death.
4. Our Lord, in conquering death, has liberated us from its fear.

The Christian's Prospect Beyond Death
Text: II Corinthians 5:8

1. The text explained — The meaning of terms "at home," "with."
   The face-to-face fellowship.
2. The text applied — The Christian will have a face-to-face experience with Christ. The experience comes immediately at death.
   The experience brings unbroken communion.

The Faded Leaf
Text: Isaiah 64:6

Introduction:
  A. A concrete illustration of the text.
  B. Human life, like the leaf, has its cycle.
  C. The emblem of all life — "all."

Proposition: To show how life fades.

I. We do all fade as a leaf in our moral life.
   A. This is the primary interpretation. Note the four analogies in the text. Morally we are like the leper who cries, "Unclean," the garment unfit to wear and unstable so that the wind drives us hither and yon.
   B. Sin shrivels and withers life.
   C. Sin creates a living death.
II. We all do fade as a leaf in our physical life.
   A. The leaf fades by a natural law — "it is appointed unto man once to die" (Hebrews 9:27)
   B. The leaf fades by a gradual process. So we fade slowly, almost imperceptibly.
   C. The leaf fades into its original element. A leaf is organized dust. So is the body of man — "Dust thou art, unto dust shalt thou return."

Conclusion:
   The fading leaf teaches us some very practical lessons:
   A. That all have the same life.
   B. That life is transient and fleeting.
   C. That old age may be beautiful.
   D. That death is certain.

The Glory of Heaven

Heaven is compared to:
   A. A Home. John 14:1-3
      Suggests familiarity and happiness.
   B. A City. Hebrews 11:10, 16; Revelation 22:14
      Suggests safety, Revelation 22:14, 15; permanency, Hebrews 11:9, 10, 16.
   C. A Country. Philippians 3:20; Hebrews 11:14, 16
      Suggests Christian fatherland, consummation of Christian pilgrimage.

The pastor will find some most helpful sermon outlines on every type of funeral in Arthur H. De Long's most excellent *Pastor's Ideal Funeral Book*, published by the Abingdon Press, in 1910, two of which we give. Here is his outline on Isaiah 64:6 which the pastor can compare with the skeleton above.

A Striking and Beautiful Symbol of Life

1. We all do fade as a leaf (Psalm 103:15, 16; I Peter 1:24). The miracle of unfolding leaves in spring — trees clothed in verdure of green all summer — with such evidences of life one might think they would never fade — Psalm 37:35-39 — yet a few frosts, and bare, naked limbs — skeletons of death, where life was so abundant — leaves scattered and gone; so man — Psalm 90:5, 6; Isaiah 40:6.

2. The utility of the leaf. While it lives — more than beautiful — necessary to life and fruitage of the tree — Psalm 1:3; Jeremiah 17:8 — It receives sap — Psalm 104:16 — Sunshine, strength, beauty of form and color. It gives life, ozone, shade, beauty, fruit —Isaiah 61:3; Luke 6:38.

3. The leaf is beautiful in death. Beholding autumnal colorings, one would think that nature had spilled her paints on the forests as she went to paint the glories of the evening sunset. So we should grow beautiful with age, for "Beauty is but the flowering of virtue." The kindly, wrinkled face and silver hair, "a crown of glory," are the fruitage of a holy life. Let blighting frosts of age and affliction come — they ripen both fruit and foliage. The gold of autumn's evening is blending with eternity's day.

4. There is a leaf that never fades — immortality. Psalm 1:3; Jeremiah 17:8; Ezekiel 47:12; Genesis 2:9; Revelation 22:2.

Frailty of Life — Death

Text: Job 30:23. "For I know that thou wilt bring me to death, and to the house appointed for all living."

1. Death is the most terrible fact in the universe. Silent, resistless (Ecclesiastes 8:8) — ruthless (Job 14:19, 20) — remorseless, stops not for medical skill, tender nursing, tears or prayers — absolute conqueror over earth (I Corinthians 15:26).

2. Death takes our friends into his cold embrace; we call, but no answer (Genesis 50:1). "Heaps of dust, but we loved them so." Our hearts rebel — but vain, we must "bury our dead out of our sight" (Genesis 23:4).

3. Soon He will take us — this we know. Inevitable (Hebrews 9:27; Ecclesiastes 9:2, 3, 8:8; Job 33:22). Comes unexpectedly (I Thessalonians 5:2).

4. Has death a conqueror? History — nature — science — infidelity say, NO. Revelation (Revelation 1:18; I Corinthians 15:55), faith (II Timothy 4:7), hope (I Peter 1:3; Psalm 23:4; Acts 7:59), experience say, YES. Death shall be conquered (Job 19:23-27; I Corinthians 15:26); No death in heaven (Revelation 21:4; 20:14; Hebrews 2:14).

Almost one hundred years ago there commenced to appear a remarkable series of ministerial helps known as *The Homilist*, edited by the two most unique men of their time — Dr. David Thomas, of London, and Urijah Rees Thomas, of Bristol. The purpose of some thirty volumes in all is stated in the preface —

> "The mission of *The Homilist* is not to supply sermons for indolent or incompetent preachers, but stimulus and tonic for the true-hearted, hard-working, and genuine teacher. It does not deal with the "ready-made," but in the raw material. It only admits contributions of the most condensed and suggestive character. It requires things, not words — healthy saplings, just rising into sight and struggling into shape, not lifeless timber, however exquisitely carved or brilliantly polished. The former may grow, the latter must rot. It prefers one life-germ to a cartload of manufactured sermons. It does not treat sacred texts as pegs on which to hang artistic discourses, but as seed-corn to be cultivated for hungry souls. *The Homilist*, in one word, proceeds upon the principle that that author serves his reader best, not who gives, but who suggests the most thought, and thus brings out from the readers' own soul thoughts and thought-producing powers of which before he was utterly unconscious."

For years these homiletical volumes enjoyed a tremendous sale. Although long out of print, a person is fortunate if he possesses any or all of the series of *The Homilist*. Being in the happy position of owning this collection, the writer felt that present-day pastors would appreciate the following eight relevant sermons prepared almost a century ago and which he has extracted for their perusal. The remaining three sermons are from the present writer's own store.

SERMON ONE

The Departure of Friends

Son of man, behold, I take away from thee the desire of thine eyes with a stroke: yet neither shalt thou mourn nor weep, neither shall thy tears run down. Forbear to cry, make no mourning for the dead, bind the tire of thine head upon thee, and put on thy shoes upon thy feet, and cover not thy lips, and eat not the bread of men. So I spake unto the people in the morning: and at even my wife died; and I did in the morning as I was commanded. (Ezekiel 24:16-18)

Friend after friend departs. Who has not lost a friend? The tenderest ties that bind man to earth are breaking every day in all circles throughout the world. "With a stroke" Ezekiel was bereft of the partner of his sorrows and joys. The passage teaches three things in relation to this subject.

1. That the departure of dear friends by death IS UNDER THE DIRECTION OF THE GREAT GOD. "Behold *I* take away." The secondary and proximate cause of death may be a cut, a blow, drowning, disease, or poison; albeit it is always under the superintendent agency of God. "Thou turnest man to destruction." "Thou changest his countenance." "Thou takest away his breath." Death is not the result of accident, necessity, or any chemical or mechanical force, but of the will of God. This doctrine teaches three practical lessons.

   a. First: That the grand aim of life *should be to please God.* Is it true that our time is in His hand, that our breath is with Him? Then should not our grand aim be to please Him in all things?

   b. Secondly: That the grand aim in bereavement should be to *acquiesce in the will of God.* He who gave and sustained life has a right to take it away. "It is the Lord: let him do what seemeth him good." "The Lord gave," etc.

    c. Thirdly: That our grand impression at every death-bed should be *that the Lord is at hand*. The writers of the Bible always speak of death in this way. They speak of it as the coming of the Lord, as the Judge standing at the door. In every funeral that darkens the street, in every open grave, at every deathbed, the Lord appears. He appears to speak with a moral thunder to the heart.

2. That the departure of dear friends by death IS THE SOURCE OF GREAT SORROW. This is implied in the command: "Yet neither shalt thou mourn nor weep, neither shall tears run down. Forbear to cry, make no mourning for the dead." The loss of a real friend is to the social heart what the amputation of a limb is to the body: great pain and great deprivation. Sorrow for the dead indicates several things.

    a. First: Something *good* in human nature. It always springs out of love, and love is divine. Had we no love for our friends we should heave no sighs and rain no tears on their graves. Quench this day all the affection that man has for man, and henceforth there will be no mourning for the dead. Sorrow is the memory of widowed affection, and nothing but a draught of utter oblivion can lap it into insensibility. This social affection is good, it is the hope of the world. Let it ebb out and humanity is undone: a mind without love is already damned. Again, sorrow for the dead indicates —

    b. Secondly: Something *wrong* in human nature. Why are the cords of friendship thus dissolved, why does that affection that is the glory of our being become our woe? Why is the sun of our nature turned into darkness, and its moon into blood? It cannot be according to the original plan of divine benevolence. The Bible gives the explanation, "As by one man sin entered into the world," etc. Man loves because he is human, man's love

turns into agony because he is sinful. Again, this
sorrow indicates —

c. Thirdly: Something *wanted for* human nature.
   What does man want to abate the sorrow?
   (1). An assurance of a happy future life.
   (2). A hope of a happy future reunion. Whence
        comes this assurance? Not from human
        speculation, philosophy, or religion, but from
        the Gospel. "I am the resurrection and the
        life," etc. "I go to prepare a place for you,"
        etc.

3. That the departure of dear friends by death SHOULD
   NOT INTERFERE WITH MORAL DUTY. "And at even my
   wife died: and I did in the morning as I was commanded." Ezekiel was sent on a mission, and though
   his wife died in the evening he continued to pursue
   his mission the next day. One might have thought
   that the event would have authorized a pause in his
   career of duty. But no, his grief, though intense, was
   not to check him. The next day found him at his place,
   with no badge of mourning but the badge that nature
   gives, viz., the sad expression of a widowed heart.
   There are three reasons why we should attend to duty
   rather than indulge in sorrow.

   a. First: Because indulgence in sorrow *confers no
      benefit on others; the fulfillment of duty does.*
      Tears and sighs and groans can never heal a broken
      heart, or chase away the clouds of ignorance from
      mind.

   d. Secondly: Because indulgence in sorrow *injures
      self, and the fulfillment of duty does good to self.*
      Sorrow injures the health, enfeebles the intellect,
      depresses the heart. Sorrow is like the midnight sky,
      under its influence all nature is depressed. The
      discharge of duty does us good. We grow morbid
      by grief, robust by work.

   c. Thirdly: Because indulgence in sorrow *does not
      suspend the claims of duty.* Duty knows no pause.

While we are sorrowing, her claims increase in number and urgency. Duty does not pause at our shrieks, accommodates not herself to our moods. Her commands are absolute, "Let the dead bury the dead."

SERMON TWO

The Gates of Death

Have the gates of death been opened unto thee? or hast thou seen the doors of the shadow of death? Job 38:17

These remarkable words are part of a wonderfully sublime address which the Infinite Maker of the universe delivered to Job amidst the rush and roar of an eastern whirlwind. The long, earnest and unsatisfactory debate which had been carried on between the patriarch and his friends touching the government of God, was thus terminated with grand abruptness. It is noteworthy, that in these communications of the Almighty, He does not condescend to propound a solution of the difficulty which had perplexed their judgment and engrossed their discussion. He gives no explanation of His doings, but the grand aim of His appeal is to impress the importance and duty of confidence in His character. Man, intellectually, is too small to comprehend His doings. A firm unshaken trustfulness therefore is at once his duty and interest.

Amongst the many things He appeals to in order to impress Job with his insignificance, as compared with his Maker, is the dark region of death expressed in the text — "Have the gates of death," etc. The allusion here is to the state which in the Hebrew is called *Sheol*, and in the Greek *Hades*. This means the dark abode of the dead — the deep, dark, vast realm to which all past generations are gone — to which the present generation is going, and whither all coming men, up to the day of doom will proceed. The ancients supposed this region to be underground, entered by the grave, and enclosed by gates and bars.

I will take this divine appeal as suggesting four things:

1. THE MENTAL DARKNESS THAT ENSHROUDS US. All the phenomena of the heavens, the earth, and the multiform operations of the Creator, referred to in this divine address, were designed and fitted to impress Job with the necessary limitation of his knowledge, and the ignorance that encircled him on all questions. And the region of death is but one of the many points to which he is directed as an example of his ignorance.

How ignorant are we of the great world of departed men! What a thick veil of mystery enfolds the whole! What questions often start within us to which we can get no satisfactory reply, either from philosophy or the Bible!

I am thankful that we are left in ignorance:

a. First: *Of the exact condition of each individual in that great and ever-growing realm.* In general, the Bible tells us that the good are happy and the wicked miserable. This is enough. We would have no more light. We would not know all about those whom we have known and loved; we would not know the *exact* pursuits they are following, and the exact thoughts and emotions that circulate in an incessant flow through their souls. If we saw them as they are, should we be fit to enjoy the few days of this brief life, or to perform its duties? We should stand, I think, paralyzed at the vision.

I am thankful that we are left in ignorance:

b. Secondly: *Of our exact proximity to the great realm of the departed.* We would not have the day or the hour disclosed. The men to whom the day of death was made known were confounded. Saul heard from Samuel, etc. Peter told Sapphira, etc.

Who, if he knew it, would undertake any enterprise? Would Moses have undertaken the guidance of the Israelites if he had known that neither he nor they would cross the Jordan? etc. Would Jonathan have ascended Gilboa? David, etc. I am thankful for the ignorance. The divine appeal suggests:

2. THE SOLEMN CHANGE THAT AWAITS US. "The gates" have not opened to us, but *must*. Speaking of death according to the figure before us we observe:

a. First: *The gates are in constant motion.* No sooner are they closed to one, than another enters. It is estimated that one enters every moment.

b. Secondly: *The gates open to all classes.* There are gates which are to be entered only by persons of distinction; but here are kings and beggars, etc.

c. Thirdly: *The gates open only one way — into eternity.* We have, it is true, an account of a few that have come back, but only one who had not to go that way again. No coming back (Job 6:7-13). "They shall," says Job, "return no more." Hezekiah. David said, "I shall go to him," etc.

I rejoice in this. I would not have the good back again — nor the bad. The Caesars, the Alexanders, the Napoleons, back again! No! Thank God for death.

d. Fourthly: *The gates separate the probationary from the retributionary.* When we pass those gates what do we leave behind? On what do we enter?

e. Fifthly: *The gates are under supreme authority.* There is only *one* Being who can open them. Not accident, etc. The divine appeal suggests:

3. THE WONDERFUL MERCY THAT PRESERVES US.

a. First: *We have always been near those gates.* We dwell in "houses of clay."

b. Secondly: *Thousands have gone through since we began the journey of life.* Younger and better too.

c. Thirdly: *We have often been made to feel ourselves near.*

(1). In personal affliction. We have felt the cold breeze coming up freezing the temple and chilling the blood.

(2). In bereavements. While we have stood by holy deathbeds we have felt the aroma wafted from the lovely scenes on the other side. "The Lord is not slack concerning his promise, as some men count slackness." The divine appeal suggests:

4. THE SERVICE CHRISTIANITY RENDERS US.

a. First: *It assures us there is life on the other side of the gates.* In stepping through them, we do not step into black extinction. The old philosophers never reached as much light as this.

b. Secondly: *It assures us there is blessedness on the other side of the gates.* It opens the door of the future and shows us a world of men in heaven. "I saw a great multitude," etc.
"They live, the beautiful, the dead,
Like stars of fire above our head."

c. Thirdly: *It takes away the instinctive repugnance we feel in stepping through those gates.* "It delivers those who through fear of death are all their lifetime subject to bondage." It takes the sting of death away, etc.

My young brethren, you, like our young friend,* must soon pass through these gates. You are very near them now. "What is your life? A vapor," etc. — the flitting rays of a meteor. With the first breath you drew you took a step toward those gates, and thither you have been wending ever since.
"Your hearts, like muffled drums,
Are beating funeral marches to the grave."

I would not lessen the pleasures of young life. I would not cool your blood, nor throw one shade over those bright and glowing prospects which imagination pictures; but I would have you take life as it is, and enjoy it for what it is worth.

*This discourse was delivered on the occasion of the death of a pious young lady who was a teacher in the Stockwell Sabbath School.

Enjoy it, as I have often enjoyed on my native mountains the setting of a summer's sun. The streaks of glory which played upon the western sky, as the great orb went down in blazing splendor, kindled within me unutterable emotions of delight, yet I felt as I admired, that the magnificent scene would soon vanish, and all above and below would be darkness.

Time, is a Prince, whose resistless sway
Everything earthly must needs obey:
The aim of war, and the tyrant's frown,
And the shepherd's crook, and the conqueror's crown,
Palaces, pyramids, temples, towers,
With the sunset's flush, and the rainbow's ray,
At the touch of Time are passing away.

SERMON THREE

Fellowship in Death

Father, into thy hands I commend my spirit. Luke 23:46
Lord Jesus, receive my spirit. Acts 7:59

I. FELLOWSHIP OF SUFFERING. They died by the hands of violent, malignant, thorough, determined foes.

II. FELLOWSHIP OF VISION. Jesus saw His Father. Stephen saw Jesus. How near is heaven to the holy! What strength and concentration of vision!

III. FELLOWSHIP OF PITY. "Father forgive them, for they know not what they do." "Lord, lay not this sin to their charge." Pitiful prayers for murderers, is the proof of divinest grace which angels have ever seen.

IV. FELLOWSHIP OF ATTITUDE. With bounding might and "loud" voices the last enemy was confronted and destroyed.

V. FELLOWSHIP OF BURIAL. Devout duty to the dead. This is the work of the living. Let us bury our friends *reverently*. They have an undying history. Let us bury our friends *sympathetically*. They ask a brother's interest. Let us bury our friends *hopefully*. They have a lasting destiny.

Lessons: (1). This precious coincidence is surely not accidental. (2). Here is a proof of the true humanity of Jesus Christ. We wonder less that Stephen was like the Saviour than that the Saviour was so like Stephen. (3). How completely one are the Lord and His people. "Thou shalt be with me." With Him heaven is not only near but accessible. (4). Fellowship with Jesus Christ in life is the surest guarantee of His presence in death.

SERMON FOUR

Death — No Respecter of Persons

Death is come up into our windows, and is entered into our palaces.
Jeremiah 9:21

The words suggest to us death as an invading enemy. As an enemy —

I. HE IS CRUEL. *He strikes at the dearest objects of our affections.* Child, husband, wife, father, mother — what names are these! How they twine themselves around our hearts; yet death, with his ruthless hand, tears them from us. He robs us of our most *useful men* — patriots, philanthropists, preachers, authors, etc. He drags us from the *dearest things of the heart,* our fields of occupation, our social circles, our cherished plans and purposes. He *reduces our bodies to the dust,* seals the senses, paralyzes the limbs, breaks up every part into its primitive dust. Cruel death! Deaf to the strongest and most piercing cries of social life.

II. HE IS UNREMITTING. He never sheathes his sword — never pauses in his march; he never bivouacs — always at work: not an hour passes that he does not strike a thousand fatal strokes. He is as restless as the sea: whoever pauses, he is active; whoever is idle, he is busy — busy in every man, in every family, in every community, in every nation — busy with all.

III. HE IS SUBTLE. He fights in ambush; he steps stealthily into the house; he touches the food, and it becomes poison; he breathes into the air, and it becomes pestiferous; he lays his hand gently on the heart, and it grows still. While his victims think themselves in the most robust health, he is instilling into their frames germs of mortal disease. He disguises himself, often appears as a most hospitable host, spreading out before men the choicest viands of earth. He works through the delicate dish and the sparkling wines.

IV. HE IS RESISTLESS. Men through ages have tried to resist him, but every effort and every expedient have failed. All that science and art and wealth and caution could do have been done a thousand times, and as often failed. The granite castles and the bodyguards of sovereigns are power-less before him. The mighty warrior who has fought and won many a battle drops his sword, falls from his horse, and becomes dust in his presence.

V. HE IS UBIQUITOUS. There is no spot on this earth where he is not at work. He is in the waves of air, and on the billows of the deep; he is in the valley and on the hill, in the mead and on the mountain. He is in the rolling river and in the rattling brook; he is in the leaves of the forest, and in the flowers of the field; he is in the fowls of the air, the creatures of the deep, and the "cattle upon a thousand hills." The whole earth is his dominion.

VI. HE IS CONQUERABLE. "The last enemy shall be destroyed." There is one who will swallow up death in victory: Christ has conquered death. (1). In His own Resurrection. (2). In His power upon the mind of His disciples. He has destroyed the fear of death in His people, so that they can triumphantly exclaim, "O Death, where is thy sting?" Death need not be a terror to us. "I congratulate you and myself," said John Foster, "that life is passing fast away. What a superlatively grand and consoling idea is that of death! Without this radiant idea, this delightful morning-star, indicating that the luminary of eternity is going to rise, life would, to my view, darken into midnight melan-choly. Oh, the expectation of living *here* and living *thus* always would be, indeed, a prospect of overwhelming despair. But thanks be to that fatal decree that dooms us to die! Thanks to that Gospel which opens the vision of an endless life and thanks, above all, to that Saviour, friend, who has promised to conduct all the faithful through the sacred trance of death into scenes of Paradise and everlasting delight."

> Teach me to live that I may dread
> The grave as little as my bed;
> Teach me to die, that so I may
> Rise glorious at the Judgment Day.
> T. Ken

SERMON FIVE

Early Graves

I will cause the sun to go down at noon. Amos 8:9

The words are suggestive of early graves, and those abound. Many babies die at birth or shortly after; children a few years older also pass away; the sun goes down just as it appears in the horizon. Those who reach threescore years and ten are a minority even in this enlightened day. Centenarians, if they exist, appear only as a solitary apple or two in the depths of winter, on a tree that was thickly clustered with fruit in the dawn of autumn. The millions that started with them are gone; they only remain, and their existence is a sadness and a warning. What do these early graves show?

I. That life is absolutely in the HANDS OF GOD. Who causes the sun to go down whilst it is yet noon? He alone can arrest its majestic progress, and turn it back. It comes forth to run its circuit, but there is One and only One who can turn it back. So it is with human life. The human creature seems organized to live on for years, but its Maker puts an end to its course at any time He pleases, so that the first breath is often immediately succeeded by the last. These early graves show —

II. That man in all stages of life should hold himself READY TO LEAVE THE WORLD. He should regard himself, not as a settler, but as a sojourner; not as a tree, to root itself in the earth, but a bark to float down the stream to sunnier shores. These early graves show —

III. That there MUST BE A FUTURE STATE for the free development of human nature. What a universe of thought and sympathy and effort are crushed in germ every year by death! Potential poets, artists, statesmen, authors, preachers, buried in early graves. Why the creation of these germs — these seeds of majestic forests? Surely the wise and benevolent Author intended their full development; and for that there must be another world.

SERMON SIX

The Shadow of Death Turned to Morning

Seek him that . . . turneth the shadow of death into the morning. Amos 5:8

In the midst of the elegy of this chapter, the strain changes; the music passes from the minor key. The prophet too bids the people turn to God — God the *Creator*, who *maketh* the seven stars; God the *Governor*, who *turneth* night to day; God the *Redeemer*, who *spoileth* the tyrant and delivers the oppressed. The Tekoan herdsman had seen every daybreak, (1) how *mightily*, (2) how *silently*, (3) how *mysteriously*, (4) how *mercifully* God brought in the brightness of day after the gloom of night. Is not this an illustration of what God is always doing?

I. He turneth WINTER to SPRING. How, when the wild flowers perfume the glen, and the foliage buds in the hedgerows, and birds carol under brightening skies, the shadow of death, that winter so often seems to be, is turned into morning.

II. He turneth ADVERSITY into PROSPERITY. Thus it was with Job. Thus need it be with many in this season of commercial depression.

III. He turneth SICKNESS to HEALTH. As with Hezekiah, "He healeth our diseases."

IV. He turneth DEATH TO IMMORTALITY. The *fear* of death He

changes into anticipation of heaven; the *memory* of the dead into realization of their blessedness; the *act* of dying into entrance into heaven.

V. He turneth PENITENCE into FAITH. So with Saul of Tarsus.

VI. He turneth SORROW into DISCIPLINE. It foretells day, even as morning does.

VII. He turneth the WORLD'S SIN AND SORROW into a GLORIOUS FUTURE. Then is "the time of the restitution of all things."

VIII. He turneth the CRUCIFIXION of Christ into INFINITE GLORY. The shadow of death on Calvary is turned into the morning of mercy and regeneration for the whole race of man. Bless the Lord who does this! Seek Him.

SERMON SEVEN

The Heaven of Humanity

And I looked, and, lo, a Lamb stood on the mount Sion, and with him an hundred forty and four thousand, having his Father's name written in their foreheads. And I heard a voice from heaven, as the voice of many waters, and as the voice of a great thunder: and I heard the voice of harpers harping with their harps: And they sung as it were a new song before the throne, and before the four beasts, and the elders: and no man could learn that song but the hundred and forty and four thousand, which were redeemed from the earth. These are they which were not defiled with women; for they are virgins. These are they which follow the Lamb whithersoever he goeth. These were redeemed from among men, being the firstfruits unto God and to the Lamb. And in their mouth was found no guile: for they are without fault before the throne of God. Revelation 14:1-5

May we not regard these verses as a pictorial representation of the *heaven of humanity?* If so, the following facts are suggested concerning the unseen realm of the good or the Christly.

I. It is a scene IN WHICH CHRIST IS THE CENTRAL FIGURE. "*And I looked* (saw) *and lo* (behold) *a* (the) *Lamb stood* (standing) *on the Mount Sion.*" No one acquainted with the Scriptures need ask who the Lamb is. Christ is the "Lamb of God." Why is Christ called the Lamb? Is it because of His innocence, or because of His moral and sacrificial character, or both? Morally He was innocent as a lamb, "holy, undefiled." "He did no sin, neither was guile found in his mouth." Or is it on account of His sacrifice? He was, indeed, a sacrifice; His whole being was a sacrifice. There have been those who have answered these questions to their own satisfaction, and there are now those who render replies without hesitation or doubt; I cannot. My eyes are too dim to penetrate into the rationale of divine operations. What seems clear is that Christ is the central figure in man's heaven. He stands on the citadel on which all eyes are fastened, and to which all hearts point and all sympathies flow.

II. It is a scene INTERESTINGLY POPULATED.

A. First: The population is very numerous. *"An hundred forty and four thousand."* This I take to be a definite number used to represent an indefinite multitude, a "multitude which no man could number." The dreamer being a Jew, his visions are of course full of Jewish facts and sentiments. Hence he thinks of the Jewish scene of worship, Sion, and the Jewish tribes, incalculably numerous. To us, however, all these are mere illustrations of things higher, more important and lasting. The human tenants in heaven were in number beyond calculation in the days of John, and they have been multiplying ever since.

B. Secondly: The population is divinely distinguished. *"His Father's name written on their foreheads."* Men glory in things that are supposed to distinguish them advantageously from their fellow men — the attractions of physical beauty, the glitter of wealth, the pomp of power; but the greatest of all distinctions, the grandest and highest, is to have the name of the Great Father manifest in our lives, written on our very *"foreheads."*

1. It is the most *beautiful* distinction. The face is the beauty of man; there the soul reveals itself sometimes in sunshine and sometimes in clouds. The beauty of the face is not in features but in expres-

sions, and the more it expresses of purity, intelligence, generosity, tenderness, the more beautiful.
How beautiful, then, to have God's name radiating
in it. God's name is the beauty of the universe.

2. It is the most *conspicuous* distinction. *"In their
foreheads."* It is seen wherever you go, fronting
every object you look at. Godliness cannot conceal
itself. Divine goodness is evermore self-revealing.
As the face of Moses shone with a mystic radiance
when he came down from the mount after holding
fellowship with God, so the lives of all godly men
are encircled with a divine halo.

3. It is the most *honorable* distinction. A man sometimes feels proud when he is told he is like some
great statesman, ruler, thinker, reformer. But how
transcendently honorable is it to bear in our face
the very image of God. Let us all seek this distinction. With the Father's "name on our foreheads"
we shall throw the pageantry of the Shahs, the
Emperors, and all the kings of the earth into
contempt.

C. Thirdly: The population is rapturously happy. *"And
I heard a voice from heaven, as the voice of many
waters, and as the voice of a great thunder: and I
heard the voice of* (the voice which I heard was the
voice of) *harpers harping with their harps; and they
sang* (sing) *as it were a new song."* All souls yonder
run into music. Here is music loud as booming billows,
pealing thunders, and melodious as the enrapturing
strains of the harp. How mean and unworthy are men's
views of religious music. "Let us sing to the glory and
praise of God," says the leader of public worship. And
forthwith the whole congregation breaks into sound.
And if the sound is regulated by the harmonious blending of notes the production is called a "service of song,"
and more, alas, is made an article of trade. Large in-
comes are made by the sale of such music. Can such
be the music of heaven? Nay. True music is the

harmony of soul, souls moving ever in accord with the Supreme will. True music consists not in a blending of sounds, whether vocal or instrumental, however charming to the senses, but in sentiments unuttered, perhaps unutterable, yet entrancing to conscience and pleasing to God.

D. Fourthly: The population is redemptively trained. *"No man could learn that song, but the hundred and forty and four thousand which were redeemed* (purchased) *from the earth."* Heaven, it has been said by men of old, is a prepared place for a prepared people. It is verily so. Observe:

1. Man requires training for heaven.
2. Redemption is the method of training for heaven.
3. Earth is the scene of this redemptive training.

E. Fifthly: The population is spotlessly pure. *"These are they which were not defiled with women; for they are virgins."* There are those of our race in heaven who have never fallen, who have retained their virgin innocence, who required no pardon for their sins, nor regeneration. What millions of the human population die in their infancy and go on unfolding their faculties and invigorating their strength through indefinite ages in scenes of absolute holiness and infallible intelligence. They were not *"redeemed from the earth,"* such redemption they required not, from the dawn of their being they were ushered into the realms of immaculate purity and perfect bliss.

F. Sixthly: The population is absolutely loyal. *"These are they which follow the Lamb whithersoever he goeth."* All follow the Lamb, the Christ of God. Two words, *"follow me,"* embody at once the whole duty and perfect paradise of souls. *"Whithersoever he goeth."* He is always moving. "The Father worketh hitherto, and I work." We cannot do exactly what He does, but we can imbibe that spirit which inspires Him in all He does. Would I become a great painter, then how shall I proceed? If I copy the exact style and method of the greatest master of the art, I shall only become a mere mechanic in the profession, never an artist. But if I catch the *genius* of the great master, I may, peradventure, leave him behind and win a place and a distinction all my own. Let us catch the moral genius of Christ.

G. Seventhly: The population is incorruptibly truthful. *"In their mouth was found no guile* (lie): *for they are without fault before the throne of God"* (they are without blemish). No lie! How unlike us! The social atmosphere of our world teems with lies as with microbes. Lies in parliaments, in markets, in churches. The whole world teems with imposters. What a blessed world must that be where all is truth and reality.

SERMON EIGHT

The Death of the Good

The righteous perisheth, and no man layeth it to heart: and merciful men are taken away, none considering that the righteous is taken away from the evil to come. He shall enter into peace; they shall rest in their beds, each one walking in his uprightness. Isaiah 57:1, 2

Whether the reference is here to King Josiah or anyone else, it matters not. The words state obvious facts in relation to the death of the good.

I. Their death is the PERISHING OF THE BODY. "The righteous perisheth." No need to prove this, no need to illustrate this. Who can misunderstand or doubt it? The earthly tabernacle rots, dust returns to dust. The bodies of all the millions of men in all the generations that have passed have perished. The greatest share the same fate.

A. Why then pamper the body?

B. Why center interests on the wants and enjoyments of the body?

II. Their death is GENERALLY DISREGARDED BY MANKIND. "No man layeth it to heart." How soon the best of men are forgotten. The death of the best, the most prominent and holy man of the age, is only as the falling of a stone into a river. There is a momentary agitation in a limited circle, but the deep stream of life rolls on, and every impression is borne away. There are two reasons for disregarding the death of the good.

A. The thought of death is repugnant to their heart.

B. The concerns of life are all-absorbing.

III. Their death is a deliverance FROM ALL THE EVILS THAT ARE COMING ON THE WORLD. "Taken away from the evil to come." What evils there have been on this earth; what evils are still to come. What boisterous oceans of agony are yet to surge over this planet? The dead are secure from it, the righteous are delivered from it. The mightiest thunders here will awaken no ripple upon their placid souls.

IV. Their DEATH IS A STEP INTO A HIGHER LIFE. "He shall enter into peace: they shall rest in their beds."

A. Their bodies sleep, "Shall rest in their beds." The death of the good as to the body is only sleep — *natural, refreshing, temporary.*

B. Their souls march on. "Each one walking in his uprightness." Endless progress. "It doth not yet appear what we shall be."

SERMON NINE

Recognition in Heaven

Then shall I know even as also I am known. I Corinthians 13:12

A friend asked George Macdonald, the Scottish novelist and poet, "Shall we know one another in heaven?" His pointed reply was: "Shall we be greater fools in paradise than we are here?" Consciousness, fellowship, love, memory, personal identity involve recognition. Each individual, *himself* or *herself* here, will possess hereafter a recognizable personality, and faculties superior to those exercised on earth. We may not have the full understanding of the *mode* of recognition in heaven, but of the *fact* there need be no doubt. Paul reminds us that heaven is the home of "the whole family in heaven and earth" (Ephesians 3:15). What kind of a home would it be if its members are to be strangers to each other forever? We can assume with certainty that we shall know one another more thoroughly in the life beyond. "Then shall I know even as also I am known" (I Corinthians 13:13). Heaven means a more holy, blessed intimacy, our present human frailties prevent.

> We shall know each other better
> When the mists have rolled away.

Further, this age-long and passionate desire has a strong sentimental value, and is likewise a perfectly legitimate one. Heaven would not be heaven, if it does not offer reunion with, and the recognition of our dead in Christ. "All love is of God," John, the "apostle of love," reminds us, and because such love cannot be buried in a coffin, the beautiful but broken relationships of earth are resumed in the Father's home above where, as members of the same family we dwell together in perfect harmony.

The Bible offers sufficient evidence of recognition among the occupants of heaven. We can be perfectly sure that the angels round about the throne of God know one another. Associated in the same service of praising the Lord, and carrying out divine behests, we must infer that these glorious spirits know each other. Surely, the two angels found sitting at the Saviour's tomb, and who announced His Resurrection, recognized one another!

Further, Old Testament saints believed that when they left earth they would join their relatives in another world and resume fellowship with them (Genesis 25:8; 35:29; 49:33). Believing that Joseph was dead, Jacob said, "I shall go down into *sheol* unto my son mourning" (Genesis 37:35). Actually, Jacob meant that he would go sorrowful into the other world there to be joined together again with Joseph. Jesus spoke about sitting down with Abraham, Isaac and Jacob in heaven. How could he do this without recognizing them? What kind of a fellowship could there be if these patriarchs have not retained their identity? (Matthew 8:11). David, as he wept over his dead child, knew that he would join him again at death. "I shall go to him" (II Samuel 12:23). Remember, David had only seen the baby

Bathsheba had borne him, but a few days, yet he believed he would distinguish their baby from the millions in heaven. David looked beyond the vast universe to the place of reunion, saying, "My child is there. I shall go to him." The value of such a hope is better understood as we remember that David, as a man after God's own heart, knew as much about the mind of God, and the nature of the other world, as almost any other Old Testament writer. Did not King Saul recognize Samuel when God permitted him to return for a few brief seconds to announce Saul's doom?

Two men came down from the glory land to have a conversation with Jesus about His death at Jerusalem. Jesus had taken three of His disciples, Peter and James and John, to the summit of a mountain, and while there the two heavenly visitants appeared, Moses who lived 1350 B.C. and Elijah 870 B.C. (Matthew 17:1-8). Peter, of course, had never seen these Old Testament saints in the flesh, yet he immediately recognized them, for he said, "Let us make three tabernacles; one for Moses, one for Elijah and one for thee." Thus their identity must have been unimpaired.

The rich man in hell recognized both Abraham and Lazarus (Luke 16:19-31). While there is much of mystery in the incident Jesus related, this much is evident, that there was unmistakable recognition. Identity had not been destroyed. Our Lord also taught that memory is immortal in the next world, for Abraham said to Dives, "Son, remember that thou in thy lifetime receivedst thy good things." In His resurrection body, Jesus retained His identity. In the twilight Mary supposed Jesus to be the gardener. To all intents and appearances He was a human being, and as soon as He spoke Mary recognized the voice — the same voice that had previously spoken to her soul. The two disciples on the road to Emmaus did not recognize Jesus for the special reason Luke explains, "Their eyes were holden that they should not know him" (Luke 24:16). But later at supper, as He broke bread, the film fell from their eyes, and they instantly recognized Him. "They knew him" (Luke 24:31). Paul would not have desired to be with Christ if he had not been sure of recognizing Him again as the One he saw on that road to Damascus (Acts 9; Philippians 1:21).

As to the righteous being able to converse with the Lord in heaven, if we can speak to Him now in prayer surely we shall be able to do so more perfectly over there? How could we be "at home" with Him and not recognize Him and be recognized by Him? "Social fellowship, so far from ceasing in heaven, will be vastly extended, and each of us will know intuitively the whole family of God. What a gathering of the ransomed that will be." If you have a dear one in heaven, your heart yearns to see, do not despair for you will meet again. The voice you loved to hear you will hear again. The identity of the one you were near to on earth remains the same, and instant recognition will be yours as you meet never to part again. Your beloved one is only "lost awhile."

One of the great thrills in heaven will be, not only that of meeting our dear ones again, but meeting the great saints of the ages, Abraham, Moses, David, Paul, and all the rest of the prophets and apostles, as well as the martyrs and the divines of the centuries, and as we meet them on the golden streets above, converse with them without restraint. As children of the same family, and all in heaven through the grace of God, introductions will be unnecessary, as we shall all meet on the common ground of relationship. The poet asks —

> Shall we know the friends that greet us
> In that glorious-spirit land?
> Shall we see the same eyes shining
> On us as in the days of yore?
> Shall we feel the dear arms twining
> Fondly round us as before?

Cardinal Newman in "Lead, Kindly Light" answers the question:

> And with the morn those angel faces smile,
> Which I have loved long since, and lost awhile.

SERMON TEN

Sorrows and Stars

> He healeth the broken in heart;
> He telleth the number of the stars. Psalm 147:3, 4

A unique feature of the Bible is its power to combine extremities. It contains a composition of opposites. For example, here are a few which could be traced with profit. *The Provision of God* is proven by the fact that He can cover the heavens with clouds, yet provide the beast with food (Psalm 147:8, 9). *The Son of God* is spoken of as the Mighty God and yet as a Babe, a combination of wonderfulness and weakness (Isaiah 9:6; Luke 2:12). The *Abode of God* is in the highest heaven and yet within the humblest heart. What extreme dwelling places! (Isaiah 57:15). *The Saint of God* is in the heavenlies and is yet to be loyal as a servant of men. He is spiritual and secular; heavenly and homely. An old writer has said that the epistle to the Ephesians begins in the heavenlies but ends in the kitchen (Ephesians 1:3; 6:5).

The Nature of God is suggested as being of a dual character in Psalm 147:3, 4, where majesty and mercy are happily combined. C. H. Spurgeon's comment on this last passage is: "We must read these two verses without a break and feel the full force of the contrast. From stars to sighs is a deep descent! From worlds to wounds is a distance which only infinite compassion can bridge. Yet He who acts a surgeon's part with wounded hearts marshals the heavenly host and reads the muster roll of suns and their majestic systems. O Lord, it is good to praise Thee as ruling the stars, but it is pleasant to adore Thee as healing the broken in heart."

What opposites are here happily wedded! Might and meekness, sovereignty and sympathy, glory and grace, stars and sighs, planets and pain, worlds and wounds, brilliant heavens and broken hearts!

A. *The Divine Character*

A close study of the psalmist's manifold description of God will deliver us from a mistaken, distorted, one-sided view of the divine character. We have, in the first place —

1. A Two-Fold Description of God.

He is revealed as the Maker of heavens and the Mender of hearts. Paul exhorts us not to mind high things but to condescend to men of low estate (Romans 12:16). God, however, can mind high things yet condescend to men and matters of low estate. On the one hand we have His greatness, in order that we might be subdued by His mighty power; and on the other hand we have His gentleness, in order that we might submit and surrender to His claim. Lofty transcendence and loving tenderness, then, walk hand in hand. God is here seen as the majestic yet merciful One. What a descent from a world of splendor above to the earth of sighs below! Why, this is the story of a Man who, although rich, yet for our sakes became poor.

We have, in the second place —

2. A Two-Fold Danger of Man.

One common danger of man is to think of God as being far too remote, distant, detached, to evince any concern over us humans. He is like the "happy land" about which we sing — "far, far away." He is too infinite to be interested in our earthly lot and lives.

The other danger is to make God too cheap, common and familiar. We overhear preachers referring to Jesus as a "good sport"! Such cheap descriptions are most unbecoming to Him who is the Lord of glory. Familiarity of this kind does indeed breed contempt.

If we are taken up exclusively with the thought of the greatness of God as the Architect of the heavens, then we fail to realize His personal care and concern. If, on the other hand, we cheapen Him, forget that He is the Lofty One, then we lose sight of His power to act in the great things of life.

A truly spiritual mind combines and harmonizes God's greatness and grace. Balance is preserved between His loftiness and love. Each side of His character is given its rightful place. Faith sees Him as the God at hand yet afar off (Jeremiah 23:23);

and these aspects of His character meet in Christ who became the God-Man. Deity and humanity flowed in the veins of Him who was ever kingly yet kind.

B. *The Divine Combination*

Guided by the Holy Spirit, the psalmist brought the stars and broken hearts together for, although they appear to be extremes, nevertheless they are alike. It is indeed delightful to trace the resemblance between the two.

1. Both are numberless!

   Stars are without number (Genesis 15:5; Hebrews 11:12). On a clear night, hundreds of stars can be discerned by the naked eye. Herschel, with the aid of a powerful telescope, counted 116,000 in less than an hour. If we could explore the regions of the sky with a perfect instrument, we might discover 1,000,000,000 stars and beyond them an unnumbered host. Thus it is with the sighs of a groaning world. Why, the world is like a vast hospital, with every home a bed! Who can count the broken hearts, sighs, tears, groans and graves? If we have the stars today, the sorrows will come tomorrow. All may be bright, merry and peaceful in our circle today — the next, the blinds are drawn, hearts are crushed by unexpected trials.

2. Some of both are undiscovered!

   The magnitude of the heavens is beyond all human calculation and conception, and perhaps beyond the grasp of angelic comprehension. Astronomers are always discovering fresh planets and locating new stars. We are always hearing of new, gigantic telescopes which will penetrate regions of space hitherto unsearched. Thus it is with crushed hearts — the majority of them are hidden from the gaze of man. Their number and causes are secret.

The greatest sufferers are the unparaded ones. Smiling faces and seemingly contented lives hide aches and pains and tragedies unheard of. The world will never learn how many broken hearts are carried in the bodies of silent martyrs.

3. Both are counted by God!

Man is unable to count the stars above and the sighs below, but God is able to tell the number of both. He is omniscient in both realms. He who numbers the stars beyond computation is likewise able to count the hairs of the head. It makes no difference to Him whether it be stars or sobs, crosses or constellations, suffering and bruised hearts or the starry and brilliant heavens. With his perfect arithmetic He is able to count both; so take courage, faint heart, the world may not know your grief, but God can count all the tiny stars of sorrow twinkling in the sky of your life.

4. Both are called by names!

God has names for all the stars, some of which are given in Scripture (Job 9:9, etc.). Many of them have been named by man. The naming of the stars by their Creator speaks of a personal interest. What a precious truth this is! If He knows the stars by name, are you not of more value than many stars? Have you not His Word — "Fear not: . . . I have called thee by thy name" (Isaiah 43:1)? He knows the street you live on, the number of your house, and the manifold cares within it. He is one of your circle, or longs to be. He singles you out, lavishes His love upon you as though you alone needed it. He knows! He loves! He cares!

5. Both are the common possession of man!

When a poor old woman saw the sea for the first time, she exclaimed, "Thank God for something there's enough of!" Well, God has been prodigal with the stars. Rich and poor alike enjoy them for no one will ever have the monopoly of the heavenly forces. Greedy men corner the necessities of life, but power will never be theirs to fence off the stars and call them their own. Taxes are demanded for all we have below; the stars, however, are still tax-free. Thus is it with our griefs, heartbreaks, sins and graves. No respect is paid to position, wealth and honor. Suffering comes alike to prince and pauper, saint and sinner.

6. Both differ in magnitude!

Paul reminds us that "one star differeth from another star in glory" (I Corinthians 15:41). With such a statement astronomers agree, for, as they can prove, the brilliant stars studding the sky do differ in their size, light and importance. Thus it is with the sorrows of man; they also vary in their nature and number. Conviction of sin, disappointed hopes, heredity, separation and death are greater for some than for others. It would seem as though some people get through life with little care, while others are loaded with adversity.

7. Both proclaim man's littleness and feebleness!

Gazing out upon the immensity of the heavens, and thinking of the sun, moon and stars, the work of God's fingers, the psalmist could do naught else but exclaim, "What is man, that thou art mindful of him?" (Psalm 8:3, 4). Why, some of the stars are billions of miles from the earth! If a bullet fired today could travel at the rate of 500 miles an hour, it would not traverse the distance in 400,500,000 years. Thus it is with the problems of life so baffling to our finite understanding. Some of the providential dealings of God are just as inexplicable as the mysteries of the stars. We cannot understand the full reason for so many "gimlet holes to let the glory through," as a child called the stars. In like manner, we must wait for the breaking of the day for an explanation of the many tears we shed.

8. Both praise God!

When the stars start singing, earth has no Hallelujah Chorus equal to the music the heavens produce. Praise Him, ye stars! (Job 38:7; Psalm 148:3). How they glorify their Creator!

> Forever singing as they shine,
> "The hand that made us is divine!"

It was so with Him who came as the Light of the world. Jesus, who will yet be seen as the Bright and Morning Star, could sing and carry a happy heart (Psalm 40:8; Mark 14:26; Numbers 24:17). Can we glory in our tribulations? Have we songs in the night? Or can it be that sorrow has silenced song? Have we learned how to fashion a ruby crown out of a rough cross? At midnight, in a dark, damp dungeon and in spite of bleeding backs, Paul and Silas could sing, sing praises unto God. Praises in a prison? Yes, this is what God can do for trusting souls.

9. Both are fashioned by God!

God made the stars! They represent the work of His perfect fingers. Man is proud of his achievements, but he has yet to fashion a star. The order, beauty, and magnitude of the stars likewise reveal a master mind. There was method at the back of their creation. Thus is it with one's cares and trials. Sometimes it is easy to sing, but difficult to believe the words —

> Every joy or trial falleth from above,
> Traced upon our dial by the Sun of Love.

It is not hard to believe that God sends our joys. We readily accept the good things of life from His loving hands, but to accept the fact that He also permits our sighs and crushing blows in order that life may become more godlike is somewhat difficult. Yet the trial of faith can result in praise — the darker the night, the more dazzling the stars. "Not a single shaft can hit till the God of love sees fit." But the shaft does hit; it is sent forth by the hand of One who cares and who in sorrow seeks His own glory and our eternal good. There is always the "nevertheless afterwards" of chastisement. The noblest life is often the product of sanctified tribulation.

C. *The Divine Consoler*

The God of the stars is the One we need for our broken hearts. Earthly physicians may be able to heal bruised bodies. Broken hearts, however, are beyond their repair. It is because He is the Maker of stars that God can mend our sorrow. The greater includes the lesser. To God great things are small, and small things are great. His power as the Creator is yours as a Comforter. He can adapt Himself to your need.

Yes, and the "broken in heart" are placed before "the stars." Suffering souls are the Lord's first thought. He is more concerned over the salvation of human lives than with the shining of heavenly luminaries. He thinks more of souls than of stars! Calvary proves this. The stars cost Him only His breath — He spake and it was done! But souls cost Him His blood — Christ died for us!

> 'Twas great to call a world from naught,
> 'Twas greater to redeem.

Two thoughts emerge from this last aspect of our meditation:

1. There is no Physician like the Creator.

   If He knows how to keep the stars in their courses, He understands your case and can meet it. Having fashioned your heart, He knows the balm to apply, seeing that it is His mission to heal (Isaiah 61:1; Luke 4:18). Are you broken in heart? Then look up into His face and pray, "O God of the stars, heal these scars of mine! Thou Creator of suns, prove Thyself to be the Cleanser of sins and the Comforter of sorrows!" He will not fail you.

2. He can heal the brokenhearted because His own heart was broken.

The Creator became the Crucified. Jesus traveled from stars to scars. The world's greatest comforters are its heaviest sorrowers. This is why the Lord is so precious (Psalm 69:20). He had to bleed before He could bless. The fingers that helped to fashion stars were ultimately nailed to a cross. Having been hurt, He can heal. He has healed many broken hearts; is He mending yours? You have His promise about being near to your crushed spirit (Psalm 34:18).

Do you doubt the interest of the Almighty One in your life? Have you learned that His greatness guarantees His graciousness; His sovereignty; His sympathy; His power; His pity; His kingliness; His kindness? Is the Lord thy Healer? Do you allow His majesty as seen in the star-be-spangled sky to awe and solemnize you? Have you discovered that He is near enough to soothe and satisfy your aching heart and to save your precious soul? If not, turn to Him now!

—H.L.

What can it mean? Is it aught to Him
  That the nights are long and the days are dim?
Can He be troubled by griefs I bear
  Which sadden the heart, and whiten the hair?
About His throne are eternal calms,
  And strong, glad music of happy psalms;
And bliss unruffled by any strife —
  How can He care for my little life?

And yet I want Him to care for me,
　While I live in this world where the sorrows be;
When the lights die down from the path I take,
　When strength is feeble and friends forsake;
When love and music that once did bless
　Have left me to silence and loneliness;
And my life song changes to sobbing prayers —
　Then my heart cries out for the God who cares.

(If the pastor has on hand a copy of the 1961 *Minister's Manual*, by Harper and Bros., New York, he will find on page 8, a different treatment altogether of the verses I have dealt with. This sermon by Dr. M. K. Heicher bears the title, *God Binds Up Our Wounds*.

SERMON ELEVEN

Three Months to Live

Set thine house in order; for thou shalt die, and not live. II Kings 20:1

Several years ago, there appeared in the *Daily Mail* of London a pathetic yet courageous document which made a solemn appeal to my heart. It was entitled "Three Months to Live" and was signed "A Man of Forty." I quote the whole text of the letter:

"If I am not mistaken, there was a picture exhibited a few years ago in which the scene was the consulting room of a physician, who was seated at his desk. Sitting in a chair opposite was a young man who had apparently received his death sentence.

"That scene was reconstructed a few days ago, I being the patient sitting opposite the specialist. Indeed, the whole scene flashed through my mind as I realized the terrible import of his words:

" 'We are not infallible, any of us, but as you have demanded the truth I will tell you. I do not think that you have more than three or four months to live. There is, of course, such a thing as Nature's miracle, but I do not advise you to rely upon such a remote possibility.'

"And my feelings? Well, it may seem strange, but after months and months of waiting and doubt there came almost a feeling of relief. I knew the worst. I had some three months' grace in which I could put my affairs in order before passing into the Great Unknown.

"Most people will think it hard for a man of forty, and with plenty of work to do, to be told that he has to go, but it has not struck me in this light. I look around me and see people suffering horribly from various diseases; they would probably welcome death; but my infirmity is not a painful one, nor will its end be painful; so, surely, things might be a lot worse.

"I shall carry on with my work just as I have done, but I shall probably extract more pleasure from the little things of life than I have done in the past. I mean such things as the beauty of the country in its summer garb, the little things one can so often do to help others, and the gambols of my little colony of cats.

"There is, however, one bitter blow. To two people only have I told my tragedy; one a business acquaintance, and the other the sweetest girl who ever breathed, and whom I had hoped to make my partner for life.

"It does seem hard to leave her, especially when, but a year ago, happiness seemed within our grasp. And she, God bless her, cheers me every day by reminding me of the possibility of a Nature's miracle; but I am not sure that this does not make it harder still, as I can see that she refuses to accept the physician's ultimatum.

"Maybe there is something in what is called woman's intuition.

"Well — I shall know, I expect, before very long."

Three months to live! What a verdict for one to hear who has just reached the prime of life! As you can see, such an ultimatum set this man thinking about a few things he proposed doing in the short span of life left to him. He is to "put his affairs in order before passing into the Great Unknown," "carry on with his work, just as he has done," "extract more pleasure from the little things of life than he had done in the past, such as the beauty of the country in its summer garb, the gambols of his little colony of cats, the doing of those little things helpful to other people."

Such a noble resolve on the part of a man who had received his sentence of death aroused similar thoughts in my own mind. I said to myself, "Suppose I had only three months to live; what would I do?" With the belief that Christ may return within the lifetime of this present generation, how ought we to spend our lives? Suppose we knew that in three months' time we should be caught up to meet the Lord in the air, as He returns for His own. How would we employ the intervening days and weeks? Some years ago, one of the British daily papers offered a prize for the best reply to the question: "How would you spend your last week on earth?" The question was occasioned by the false and foolish prediction by a businessman that the Lord would be here on the 12th of June, 1933.

The result of my meditation is the present message.

Several Bible saints who knew, within an hour almost, the time of their departure, flashed across my mind. There is Moses who, after being told of the lonely grave he would fill upon Mount Nebo, prayed, as he thought of his remaining days among the people: "Teach us to number our days." There is Paul who, if legend be true, died by the hand of an executioner and who apparently knew, just as a murderer knows, the exact hour when his spirit would be dismissed. Yet with calm confidence Paul faced eternity, saying, "I am now ready to be offered."

There is our Lord Jesus, who knew that His hour had come and who, with the shadow of Calvary over His heart, could pray, "Father, the hour is come; glorify thy Son, that thy Son also may glorify thee!"

It is an inspiration to turn to the Bible and read over the experiences of those who, from the Great Physician, received their summons to depart this life. See how they filled the little while between the reception of the solemn verdict of death and its execution, and "go thou and do likewise!"

Three months to live! Here are some things I would strive to do if I knew that I had only so short a period on earth before passing the way of all flesh or being caught up to meet my Lord.

A. *I Would Examine My Heart Life.*

Such an examination is necessary in order to ascertain whether I am ready to go hence — whether I am absolutely right with God — for it is the height of folly to face such a near exit without being prepared for eternity.

The writer of the letter we have quoted meant to "put his affairs in order before passing out into the Great Unknown." We trust this included his affairs Godward, as well as manward, and that his last three months on earth — unless he encountered one of Nature's miracles — brought to him the absolute certainty of sins forgiven and of a heart made ready for the other side. Then eternity would have brought to him not the Great Unknown, but the Great Known, even the Father's house with its many mansions.

King Hezekiah, you will remember, received a similar verdict. Said the prophet Isaiah to him: "Thus saith the Lord, set thine house in order, for thou shalt die and not live." How did Hezekiah receive this ultimatum? He turned his face to the wall, and prayed. The fulfillment of the decree was held in abeyance for fifteen years, not by a miracle of Nature but by the will of God.

My friend, if you knew that you had only three months to live, could you say that all your spiritual affairs are in order — that Jesus has already entered the disorder and confusion caused by sin, and has made you ready for your translation? Do not forget that you may have only three months to live or, it may be, only three weeks, three days, three minutes. No one has any lease on life. The present moment is the only one we can claim.

Although you have not sought the advice of a physician, you might be doomed to die as was this young man of forty. It has been said that we all carry about with us the seeds of trouble that will bring about our death. Canon Liddon, in one of his remarkable sermons, said: "Already, it may be, the strongest man in this cathedral carries within himself the secret, un-suspected mischief that will in time display itself as fatal disease and will lay him in his grave."

That oft-recurring headache may be the tapping that will give a final blow to your brain, thus giving you a hurried dispatch into eternity. That continual cough may be Nature's red signal of the coming danger of closed lungs and loss of breath. That persistent, gnaw-ing pain may be the warning of a foul disease which, like the arms of an octopus, will increase its grip until death releases you. That blood pressure, those swollen veins are probably the forerunners of that day not far distant when the silver cord will be loosed, the golden bowl or the pitcher broken at the fountain, or the wheel broken at the cistern — which is Solomon's descriptive way of stating those most common complaints known as heart failure and the bursting of blood vessels.

The question is, whether death comes suddenly or after a protracted illness — naturally or tragically, soon or late — are you ready to meet God? If not, then, ere pain and disease deaden your consciousness, get right with Him by accepting Jesus Christ as your own per-sonal Saviour. If the Master should return in three months' time, would you be ready to meet Him?

B. *I Would Examine My Personal Life.*

If, with only three months to live, death, or the coming of the Lord, would present no terrors, seeing that I have the assurance of a soul saved from sin and hell through the blood of the Lamb, I should feel it incumbent upon me to examine every part of my personal life, in order to discover how I would mend my way.

1. I would think of the habits I could cast off. Habits that waste time and money, that are useless, without nobility and are harmful to the body, as well as dishonoring the Lord, would be put in the place of death. I would make these three months the great-est period of sanctification ever experienced.

2. I would think of the debts I should settle. It brings dishonor upon the cause of Christ when a Christian dies leaving debts either to be cancelled by creditors or paid by friends. Beloved, because we may die, or vanish, at any moment, let us strive to have our testimony.

3. I would think of the estrangements I should repair. Let me seek out those who have wronged me, or whom I have grieved, so that we may put things right. Have I brothers and sisters, relatives, fellow Christians, from whom I am severed as the result of some petty quarrel? Then, while my life lasts, let me exhibit the forgiving spirit of Calvary. I may die, or rise to meet my Lord, tomorrow. What then? Let me not delay to write the letter, or speak the word, which will heal the breach.

4. I would think of the sunshine I could scatter. This man of forty years, with only three months to live, tells us that in such an allotted span he meant to extract more pleasure out of life by doing those things that one can do to help others.

   I would follow his example. I would examine my bank book and make sure that I had made the best possible provision for my loved ones. This, of course, is my first duty according to Scripture: "But if any provide not for his own, and specially for those of his own house, he hath denied the faith, and is worse than an infidel" (I Timothy 5:8). Then I would think of all that I could do in three months to bring blessing to a few poor, needy souls. If I were to see my Lord so soon, it would please His heart to know that I had sought to change my spare gold into the current coin of loving thought and kindness.

   I could not allow greed to characterize my remaining days. If I take a greedy, miserly heart to heaven with me, I shall want to snatch the gold from its shining streets, since it will pain me to see it under my feet!

C. *I Would Examine My Christian Life.*

If I am a Christian as the result of a definite transaction uniting me to Christ, if I am accepted in the Beloved and thereby justified freely from all things, even such a stupendous work of grace does not nullify my physical dissolution. If Christ tarries, I have to die, even as the worst sinner upon earth has to die.

Being a Christian does not absolve me from death, unless, of course, my Lord returns for me by way of the air. Therefore if, as a Christian, I have only three months to live, let me determine to get the utmost out of my spiritual privileges. Let me redeem the time by filling the passing hours with service bearing the stamp of the divine.

1. I would make my life more prayerful and holy. Three months to live! Then let me live them in the presence of God, agonizing for the deepening of my own spiritual life and for the development of the Master's image in all my days. Let me die to all self-pleasing, self-thought and self-satisfaction, and let me seek a life radiant with the glory of my Lord. Let me live so close to heaven that a breath would waft me there.

2. I would be active, virile and self-sacrificing in His cause. Numbering my days, I would apply my heart unto heavenly wisdom, even unto the wisdom of winning souls (Proverbs 11:30). Loved ones are still unsaved; children, parents, relatives and friends are still outside the fold. My lips will soon be silent. The grave, or my translation, will close my testimony. Therefore let me rescue the perishing and care for the dying by warning them with tears to seek the Lord while He may be found.

3. I would be obedient to every command of His. If

the time of my departure is at hand, I would endeavor to fulfill every command the Saviour enforces.

He told me to eat the bread and drink the wine as an act of loving remembrance of Him, until He comes. Well, if He is coming for me by way of the grave or the clouds, let me grasp every convenient opportunity of sitting at His table, thus remembering His dying love.

He, the loving, sinless Lord, went down into Jordan's waters and left me an example that I should follow His steps. Have I submitted myself to the waters of baptism, as a symbol of identification with Him in death, burial and resurrection? Then let me not forget the significance of such a holy rite. Have I not obeyed and followed my Lord thus? Then let me not hesitate to obey, as I do not want to meet the baptized Christ with disobedience upon my heart. Through His servant Paul, He commands me to be filled with the Spirit. Only three months to live! Then well might I pray: "O Lord, may they be months of Pentecostal fullness when out of me there shall flow rivers of living water!"

4. I would seek to live calmly and sweetly for God amid the duties and obligations of life. Our friend who received the physician's ultimatum regarding the length of his sojourn here remarked, "I shall carry on with my work just as I have done." What a noble resolution! Such a courageous spirit must have enabled him to die well.

Something of this same devotion is found in John Wesley's life. A lady once asked him, "Suppose that you knew you were to die at twelve o'clock tomorrow night. How would you spend the intervening time?"

"How, madam?" he replied. "Why, just as I intend to spend it now. I should preach this evening at Gloucester, and again at five tomorrow morning; after that I should ride to Tewksbury, preach in the afternoon and meet the societies in the evening. I should then repair to Friend Martin's house, who expects to entertain me, converse and pray with the family as usual, retire to my room at ten o'clock, commend myself to my heavenly Father, lie down to rest, and wake up in glory."

Friends, we may have a shorter time than three months to live. Whether the period be short or long, let us not moan or despair, especially if we have any intuition regarding our end. Let us face the duties and obligations at home, the difficulties and cares of business, the monotonous tasks of our daily toil, with brave, believing hearts.

If you are saved by grace, all is well. When your last night comes, you can lay yourself down upon your bed for a peaceful sleep and wake up in the land where the roses never fade, where there is no disease, and no death.

— H. L.

SUPPLEMENTARY READINGS

Broadus, John *The Preparation and Delivery of Sermons* (Harper, New York) 1944

De Long, Arthur H. *Pastor's Ideal Funeral Book* (Abingdon, Nashville) n.d.

English, John M. *The Minister and His Ministry* (Judson Press, Philadelphia) 1924

Heicher, M. K. *Minister's Manual 1961* (Harper, New York) 1961

Mark, Harry C. *Patterns for Preaching* (Zondervan, Grand Rapids) n.d.

4

BENEFICIAL AIDS AND EXAMPLES

Of Prayers

Because of the subduing, soothing, uplifting efficacy of prayer, it is imperative for the pastor to give much thought to intercession for the sick, the dying and the bereaved. He, himself, must endeavor to live in close, unbroken contact with the God of all comfort. It is only then that his prayers for the needy will contain the elements of "quietness, application, reach and the language of religion." Speaking long to God before he goes out to stand as an intercessor, the pastor will possess that concentration of thought, commanding the attention of a dying person, as well as that of those who gather at the funeral after death has come. Cabot and Dicks, in dealing with prayer and the dying, and with mourners, remind us that —

> "All prayer should be cast in the language of the Bible, which contains religion at its best, especially in the gospels, in several of the epistles, and in the Psalms. We frequently include a Scriptural verse to be certain that the strength of religious language is brought to the person's mind. In this respect the Prayer Book has advantages. The language of religion is best in its poetry; it is simple, straightforward, rich in meaning and association. It suggests dignity, patience and fortitude."

Cabot and Dicks, in the examples they enumerate from the Anglican Prayer Book, cite the following offered when a dying saint requested prayer that she might die that night —

Eternal Father, hear this humble prayer of gratitude:
Wouldst Thou, in Thy great mercy and affection
Take this one unto Thyself!
Relieve her from the pain and the weariness.
For her great courage and endurance we are truly thankful;
In the quiet of the night may she go unto Thee,
And in her going may she not regret leaving her loved ones;
May she know that they will come presently,
For we are all soon to follow.
But if it be not Thy will that she may come unto Thee
    tonight,
Give her strength to complete the race so nobly thus far run:
The grace of the Lord Jesus be with thee,
The communion of the Holy Spirit upon thee,
The love of God possess thee,
And give thee peace.

Amen

* * *

That heartfelt prayer can come as healing balm to bruised hearts
in the dark hours of life can be gathered from these further
"prayers," which we have lighted upon, all of which can guide
the pastor in his own intercessory ministry. We heartily commend that unique volume Peter Marshall has given us of his
prayers (*The Prayers of Peter Marshall*) containing intercessions
for all occasions. No pastor should be without this rich, spiritual
classic. Here are five of those moving prayers that must have
touched many hearts —

In Time of New Bereavement

Father, eyes blinded by the symbols of sorrow cannot see the
stars. Even so, I, at this moment, can see nothing beyond my
own grief.

I have been face to face with misery and loneliness in these
days; with the strangeness of life and death that takes away a
loved one and gives no explanation; with the mystery of a Providence I have tried to understand and cannot understand.

Thou, O Holy Spirit, Thou visitor in sorrow, Thou who art

acquainted with human tears and broken hearts, sorely I need Thy help now.

Because my heart is sore, I have shut the door of my heart to my fellows, even to Thee. But I sense that withdrawal and the effort to dull my feelings is not the way toward healing. Help me now to dare to open my being wide to the balm of Thy loving Spirit, unafraid of any depth or height or intensity of overflowing emotion.

>Thou hast promised to wipe away all tears from our eyes.
>I ask Thee to fulfill that promise now.
>Thou hast promised to bind up our wounded spirits.
>I ask Thee to fulfill that promise now.
>Thou hast promised to give us peace, not as the world gives but in the midst of our trouble.
>I ask Thee to fulfill that promise now.
>Thou hast promised to be with us alway.
>I therefore thank Thee that Thou art walking beside me every step of the way.

I put my hand in Thine, and walk on into the future, knowing that it will be a good future because Thou art in it.

Amen

* * *

For a Friend With a New Grief

Our Father, we think of that inner room of a family's sorrow into which only Thou canst truly enter.

Though all our sympathy goes out to these, our friends, we know that sympathy cannot bind up the broken heart. Only Thou canst do that. We ask Thee now to perform that gracious and healing ministry.

And help her who walked by his side — in this hour of grief and parting — to rededicate herself to Thee in a way that shall bring to her troubled heart Thy promised joy and peace.

In His name, who conquered death, we make this intercession.

Amen

* * *

For Loneliness in Bereavement

Father, I am only human, I need the touch of human companionship. Sorely I miss those I love who are with Thee.

I pray, O Jesus, that Thou wilt reveal to me unseen presences. Help me to know how close my loved ones are. For if they are with Thee, and Thou art with me, I know that they cannot be far away.

> Make real for me that contact of spirit with spirit that will re-establish the lost fellowship for which my heart yearns.
> Give to me faith shining through my tears.
> Plant peace and hope within my heart.
> Point me with joy to the great reunion.

But until then, enable me to live happily and worthily of those who are with Thee. In the Name of Him who is the Lord of Life, I pray.

Amen

* * *

For One Who Will Not Be Comforted

Father, we join our prayers in asking Thy help for this one, who bereaved, still feels lonely. He has not even yet found the joy of Thy Resurrection and the sense of the presence of the one he loves who is with Thee.

Grant that he may feel her near, may somehow be persuaded that she still lives, that she is happy, that she still loves him as he loves her.

May such assurances come to all the hearts that need them today. We ask in the name of our Lord.

Amen

* * *

For Those Who Bear a Living Grief

Lord Jesus, Thou hast been despised and rejected of men; be merciful to the disillusioned, to all those whose hearts have been wounded.

There are some for whom skies are dark, whose future is uncertain. These are Thy children with nameless griefs, weighed down in the bitterness of sorrow, living sorrows that have no graves and cannot be buried. There are hearts heavy with suspense, who wait in the twilight of an excruciating uncertainty.

Thou art a God who knowest every sin and shame of our lives and who loves us still. Be gracious now unto all these. Make them to feel the strength and the power of Thy grace that grants the ability to endure.

But, Lord, we pray not just that they will endure. We ask that even as a grain of sand in the oyster shell becomes — by patience and the grace of God — a pearl, so may the troubles of these, Thy children, yet become tokens of loveliness to glorify Thee. May they learn through those troubles what a wonderful God Thou art! Then shall we lift up our hearts, for Thou shalt cause a new light to shine in their eyes and a lilting song to return to their jaded hearts.

We know, Lord, that at the last all the lost chords of earth will be found in heaven; all the broken melodies of our lives will be blended in the harmony and beauty of Thy glory. By this hope are we upheld and sustained; in this hope we live. In the strong name of Jesus Christ, our Lord.

Amen

* * *

Another excellent compilation of prayers for every conceivable occasion is that fascinating and comprehensive work *A Chain of Prayer Across the Ages,* compiled and arranged by Selina F. Fox. This monumental work is one of the finest treasuries of prayers we know of. From various sources these are suggested for "a death in the home."

> We commend unto Thee all those about to depart this life, beseeching Thee to grant unto them the spirit of tranquility and trustfulness. May they put their hope in Thee and having passed through the valley of the shadow in peace, may they enter into the rest that remaineth for the people of God; through Jesus Christ our Lord.
>
> *Amen*

* * *

May we become as this little child who now follows the Child Jesus, that Lamb of God, in a white robe whithersoever He goes: even so, Lord Jesus. Thou gavest him (or her) to us; Thou hast taken him (or her) from us. Blessed be the name of the Lord. Blessed be our God for ever and ever.

Amen

* * *

O Lord, we remember with thanksgiving, this dear one Thou hast taken to be with Thyself. Grant us grace to follow Thee to the end. May we never look back, nor err from the way; but hasten to Thee without stumbling, finally to attain eternal blessedness with all Thy saints; through the merits of Thy Son, our Lord Jesus Christ, unto whom, with Thee, and the Holy Spirit, be the glory and praise, both now and evermore.

Amen

* * *

For those who weep and mourn over the separations death causes we have these prayers —

O most loving Saviour, let the cry of widows, orphans, and destitute children enter into Thine ears. Comfort them with a mother's tenderness, shield them from the perils of this world, and bring them at last to Thy heavenly home.

Amen

* * *

Heavenly Father, hear our voice out of the deep sorrow which Thou in Thy mysterious wisdom hast brought upon us. We know that Thou art with us, and that whatsoever cometh is a revelation of Thine unchanging love. Thou gavest and Thou hast taken away, blessed be Thy Name. O keep our souls from all temptations of this hour of mourning, that we may neither sorrow as those without hope, nor lose our trust in Thee; but that the darker this earthly scene becometh, the lighter may be our vision of that eternal world where all live before Thee. And grant that the remnant of this our family, O Lord, still being upon earth, may be steadfast in faith, joyful through hope, and rooted in love, and may so pass the waves of this troublesome world, that finally we may come to the land of everlasting life, there to reign with Thee, world without end, through Jesus Christ our Lord.

Amen

* * *

Philipp Melanchthon, 1497, friend of Martin Luther, left us this brief petition for all those in sorrow —

Comfort, O merciful Father, by Thy Word and Holy Spirit all who are afflicted or distressed, and so turn their hearts unto Thee, that they may serve Thee in truth, and bring forth fruit to Thy glory. Be Thou, O Lord, their succor and defense: through Jesus Christ our Lord.

Amen

* * *

For Armistice Day, or Remembrance Day if observed on a Sunday, the following prayers and benedictions may serve to stimulate thoughts as the pastor prepares, not only his message but also his intercessory prayer —

O God, our heavenly Father, we bless Thee again for the remembrance of this day, when by Thy providence, and by the might of Thine arm, Thou madest wars to cease; accept our praise and thanksgivings.

As on this day we remember before Thee all those who fought and died that we might live, accept our gratitude, and make us, we humbly beseech Thee, more worthy of their sacrifice even unto death, and help us to follow more closely in the steps of Thy blessed Son, that at last, we with them, may stand in Thy presence, where with the Father and the Holy Ghost, all praise, thanksgiving, honor and might be ascribed, world without end.

Amen

* * *

We bless Thy holy Name, O God, for all Thy servants who, having finished their course, do now rest from their labors. Give us grace, we beseech Thee, to follow the example of their steadfastness and faithfulness, to Thy honor and glory, through Christ Jesus our Lord.

Amen

* * *

In remembrance of those who made the great sacrifice, O God, make us better men and women, and give peace in our time, through Jesus Christ, Thy Son, our Saviour.

Amen

* * *

Almighty and everlasting God, we give Thee humble thanks for the memory and good example of Thy servants who have laid down their lives in the service of our country. We bless Thee for their courage and devotion. Accept their sacrifice we pray Thee. Let it not be in vain that they have died in the cause of righteousness and honor. And of Thy mercy, O heavenly Father, vouchsafe that we, who now serve Thee here on earth, may at last, together with them, be found meet to be partakers of the inheritance of the saints in light, for the sake of Jesus Christ Thy Son, our Lord and Saviour.

Amen

* * *

As we bless Thy holy Name for those Thy servants departed this life in Thy faith and love, so we beseech Thee to give to us who remain, grace to follow their good example, and to carry on the work which they began. Grant, O Lord, we pray Thee, that the offering of their lives may not have been made in vain; that we and all Thy people may hear the call to nobler living which sounds in our ears from the graves of those who have died, that we might live; that we may dedicate our lives anew to the work of bringing in Thy Kingdom upon earth; that so out of these years of sin, and misery and loss, there may arise a better world through Jesus Christ our Lord.

Amen

* * *

Remember, O Lord, what Thou hast wrought in us and

not what we deserve; and, as Thou hast called us to Thy service, make us worthy of our calling; through Jesus Christ our Lord.

Amen

* * *

O Father of Spirits, we have joy at this time in all who have faithfully lived, and in all who have triumphantly died. We thank Thee for all fair memories and all aspiring hopes, for the sacred ties that bind us to the unseen world, for the dear and holy dead who encompass us like a cloud of witnesses, and make the unseen heaven a home to our hearts. May we be followers of those who through faith and patience now inherit the promises. In this hour of quiet thought and solemn joy, may the meditation of our hearts and the answer of our lips be from Thee, through Jesus Christ our Saviour, who is the Resurrection and the Life.

Amen

* * *

O God, the strength of those who suffer, and the repose of them that triumph, we rejoice in the communion of saints. We remember all who have faithfully lived, all who have passed on into heaven (especially those most dear to us). May we have the assurance of their continual fellowship in Thee, and realize that though converse be no longer possible according to the flesh, there is no separation in the realm of love. Lift us into that light and love, where the Church on earth is one with the Church in heaven; through Jesus Christ our Lord.

Amen

* * *

O God, our heavenly Father, we would especially remember before Thee on this day of remembrance all those who have suffered and been maimed, disabled or blinded — those whom the war has left weakened in body or mind. Grant that they may never be forgotten, but that they may live brave, cheerful, and so far as may be, useful lives amid grateful regard and deserved honor. Give them, O Lord, Thy peace and the abiding sense of Thy sustaining power, and enable us, each one, to do our part for their comfort and help, through Him who is the Burdenbearer, even Jesus Christ, Thy Son, our Lord.

Amen

*   *   *

O God of all mercy and comfort, accept the heartfelt praises and thanksgivings of those whose dear ones, after having fought a good fight, returned to them in safety. In the greatness of their joy may they ever be mindful of those whose lives are shadowed with abiding sorrow, for the sake of Christ Jesus our Saviour.

Amen

*   *   *

O God our Father, on this day of remembrance, look upon the unrest of the world and be pleased to complete the work of Thy healing hand. Send peace upon the earth, a deeper and more lasting peace than the world has ever known. Draw all men unto Thyself, and to one another by the bonds of love. Grant understanding to the nations with an increase of sympathy and mutual good will, that they may be united in a sacred brotherhood wherein justice, mercy and faith, truth and freedom may flourish, so that the sacrifice of those who died may not have been made in vain, for the sake of Christ Jesus our Lord.

Amen

*   *   *

Prayers for the Dead

While pastors of Protestant and evangelical churches reject such an aspect of intercession, yet because the matter may occasionally arise we feel it may be helpful for a pastor to have necessary guidance if approached by hearts anxious about prayer contact with their departed.

A problem concerning some bereaved hearts is whether those who have passed from their personal care and influence can be helped by constant intercession for them. Roman Catholicism teaches that there is a purgatory where souls not bad enough for hell and not holy enough for heaven enter, and that prayer, money and masses can help them out of purgatory into heaven. Martin Luther, the one-time Roman Catholic monk said, "Since Scripture does not say anything about prayers for the dead, I do not concede it a sin if a man in his private devotions prays in terms like this: 'Dear Lord, if it is the case that this soul can be helped, then do Thou graciously etc.,' and when this has been done once or twice let that suffice." J. Paterson Smyth, in his volume, *The Gospel of the Hereafter*, relates this story a friend told him: "I was a little child when the news came of my father's death, far away. That night, as usual, I prayed for him. But my aunt stopped me. 'Darling,' she said, 'you must not pray for Father now; it is wrong.' And I can remember still how I shrank back, feeling as if someone had slammed the door and shut Father outside." One of our poets has expressed a similar desire to surround the departed with our prayers in these lines —

> How can I cease to pray for thee? Somewhere
> In God's wide universe thou art today.
> Can He not reach thee with His tender care?
> Can He not hear me, when for thee I pray?
> Somewhere thou livest and hast need of Him,
> Somewhere thy soul sees higher heights to climb,
> And somewhere, too, there may be valleys dim
> Which thou must pass to reach the heights sublime.
> Then all the more because thou canst not hear
> Poor human words of blessing, will I pray
> O true, brave heart, God bless thee, whereso'er
> In God's wide universe thou art today.

But while Scripture has much to say about prayer and intercession, it gives no sanction whatever for prayers for the dead. Our eternal destiny is fixed before we pass over, and no one and nothing can change that destiny. The person we die, whether saved or unsaved, that person we are on the other side forever. For our dear ones who died in Christ all is well. They are with Him and safe in His care and keeping, and require no prayers of ours to help them. For those who died without Christ as their Saviour, prayers from this side cannot avail them. As Professor Wm. Clow puts it: "Beyond the fact that there is no record of prayer for the dead, there is the more conclusive fact that everywhere death is regarded as a change so decisive that the opportunities of life are closed finally and forever . . . . We cannot build a doctrine upon the feelings and desires of men. We cannot pray without knowledge, and any knowledge of the state of the dead is beyond our power."

But while Scripture says nothing about prayers for the dead, does it not enlighten us on the question of the dead praying for the living? There are a few references in the Book of Revelation to the prayers of saints who have gone on before —

> "Golden vials full of odours, *which are the prayers of saints.*"
> "He should offer it *with the prayers of all saints* upon the golden altar which was before the throne. And the smoke of the incense which came *with the prayers of the saints.*"
> "I saw under the altar the souls of them that were slain . . . and *they cried,* How long, O Lord, holy and true, dost thou not judge and avenge our blood on them that dwell on the earth?" (Revelation 5:8; 8:3, 4; 6:9, 10).

Believing, as we do, that the Revelation given to John was a divine one, we have no hesitation in affirming that the passages above offer clear evidence that the saved departed can, and do, pray for us, even as Christ Himself in heaven prays for us (Romans 8:34; Hebrews 7:24, 25; I John 2:1). While on the earth, those dear saints had us constantly in their prayers, and although no longer here, they continue such a gracious ministry on our behalf. And we owe more than we realize to the prayers of these unseen saints, whose very intercession implies a degree of knowledge and memory.

The Early Fathers had much to say on this question of departed saints praying for us. Origen, one of the most eminent of the early Christian writers after the apostles, who has been referred to as "the father of Biblical criticism and exegesis in Christendom" wrote —

> "It will not be out of place to say that all the saints who have departed this life, still retaining their love for those who are in the world, concern themselves for their salvation, and *aid them by their prayers and meditation* with God."

In support of his statement Origen quotes II Maccabees 15:14 —

> "This is Jeremias the prophet of God who always prays for the people."

It was also Origen who encouraged Ambrose not to shrink from martyrdom through fear of leaving his family unbefriended. After death, "you will have greater power to help them, and will pray for them with greater wisdom."

We may not have the unquestionable warrant for making an agreement with our loved ones such as Cyprian and his friend Cornelius made. These two saintly souls anticipating the pain of separation, agreed that the first to be taken should remember in prayer those who were left behind. Their loving covenant read —

> "Let us mutually be mindful of each other, with one heart and with one mind. On both sides let us always pray for each other, let us relieve our afflictions and distresses by a reciprocity of love, and whichever of us goes hence before the other by the speed of the divine favor, let our affection continue before the Lord, *let not prayer for our brothers and sisters cease before the mercy of the Father.*"

Gregory Nazianzen in his *Funeral Oration on Basil* said:

> "He now abides in heaven, and there, as I think . . . *prays* for the people, for he did not so leave us, *as to have left us altogether.*"

That Gregory believed in the continuity of life, of love, and of intercession is further evidenced when speaking of his departed father he said:

> "I am satisfied that he accomplishes — *now by his prayers* more than he did before by his teaching, just in proportion as he approaches nearer to God, after having shaken off the fetters of the body."

Augustine, who became known as "The Doctor of Grace," has this passage expressing his belief in the prayers of the dead:

"May Cyprian help us with his prayers for us who are toiling in this mortal flesh as beneath some murky cloud, so that if the Lord grant it, we may to the best of our ability copy his virtues."

Of Poems and Hymns

John Keble, the English cleric and poet (1792-1866), who gave to the Church some of its most treasured spiritual poems affirmed that, "Verse has more power to soothe than prose" and that, "the glorious art of poetry is a kind of medicine divinely bestowed upon man." In his Latin *Lecture on Poetry*, translated by E. Kershaw Francis, Keble has this Dedication to another poet —

"To William Wordsworth, the true philosopher and inspired poet, who by special gift and calling of Almighty God, whether he sang of man or of nature, failed not to lift up men's hearts to holy things."

It is because of this healing and inspiring influence of expressive poetry that the pastor should have on hand a selection of relevant poems as he comes to bury the dead and console the bereaved. We trust the following specimens will prove serviceable.

At the funeral of John Neale, of whom Archbishop Trench said, "He is the most profoundly learned hymnologist of the Church," his friends sang a special favorite of his for its music's sake. This first verse could be used in the funeral sermon at the burial of an aged person —

> Safe home, safe home, in port!
>   Rent cordage, shattered deck,
> Torn sails, provisions short,
>   And only not a wreck;
> But oh! the joy upon the shore,
> To tell our voyage — perils o'er.

* * *

In her old age, Anna L. Barbauld, daughter of a dissenting minister, who was eminently successful as a writer of hymns, wrote the following stanza, which poet Rogers regarded as one of the finest verses in English literature. Henry Crabbe Robinson repeated it to Wordsworth and heard him say:

"I am not in the habit of grudging people their good things, but I wish I had written those lines."

Here they are —

> Life! we have been long together
> Through pleasant and through cloudy weather;
> 'Tis hard to part when friends are dear, —
> Perhaps 'twill cost a sigh, a tear;
> Then steal away, give little warning,
> Choose thine own time;
> Say not, "*Good night;*" but in some brighter clime
> Bid me, "*Good morning.*"

* * *

Quoting these lines at the burial of an aged person, the pastor could also add what old Thomas Fuller, the renowned English divine, said to his nephew, James Cuthbert, in his last moments —

"Good night, James — but it will soon be morning!"

* * *

As any preacher knows, John's description of heaven is made up of a few "no more's," and Julia Sterling embodies these negatives in these comforting lines which could be effectively used in a message on heaven.

> The Home beyond the shadows
> Hath neither pain nor tears;
> But, through its cloudless regions
> The Light of Life appears —
> Dispelling ev'ry sorrow,
> Removing ev'ry care,
> And giving rest eternal
> To all who enter there.
> Far beyond the shadows
> Through the gates that never close,
> There the King Himself will lead us
> Where the living water flows.

* * *

Dean Alford, the renowned theologian gave utterance to the same hope in his verse —

> Oh, then with raptured greetings
> On Canaan's happy shore,
> What knitting severed friendships up,

Where partings are no more!
Then eyes with joy shall sparkle
That brimmed with tears of late,
Orphans no longer fatherless,
Nor widows desolate.

* * *

The Bible does not open the door on any second chance beyond the grave. Dying without hope or faith, we remain without hope eternally. Such finality is indicated by J. J. Simms thus —

The tide is flowing out,
And we upon its bosom borne
Are drifting to the sea;
Drifting out to darkness, far from love and light
Where the storms are raging, into endless night;
Or drifting on to glory, past all pain and care,
Into heaven's brightness, where the ransomed are.

* * *

The entire poem of J. L. McCreery, of which we cite two verses, is likewise applicable for any type of funeral service —

There is no death! the stars go down
To rise upon some fairer shore,
And bright in heaven's jeweled crown
They shine for evermore.

They are not dead! they have but passed
Beyond the mists that blind us here,
Into the new and larger life
Of that serener sphere.

* * *

Is not the idea of death as the striking of a tent, which John Oxenham sets forth in verse, appealing?

Fold up the tent! the sun is in the West;
This house was only lent,
For my apprenticement,
And God knows best,
Fold up the tent!
Its pole all broken, and its cover rent,
Its work is done.

* * *

Robert Burns, the Scottish bard, left a few gems, to which a pastor can give a setting in his message for mourners. We have the sublime and affecting Ode he wrote on the anniversary of Highland Mary's death, the second verse of which reads —

> That sacred hour can I forget,
>   Can I forget that hallowed grove,
> Where by the winding Ayr we met,
>   To live one day of parting love!
> Eternity cannot efface
>   Those records dear of transports past;
> Thy image at our last embrace;
>   Ah! little thought we 'twas our last!

* * *

Then there is the further poem of Burns on "A Mother's Lament for the Death of Her Son," that a preacher might find applicable for the funeral of a child, or young person —

> Fate gave the word, the arrow sped,
>   And pierc'd my darling's heart;
> And with him all the joys are fled
>   Life can to me impart.
> By cruel hands the sapling drops
>   In dust dishonor'd laid;
> So fell the pride of all my hopes,
>   My age's future shade.

* * *

With a volume of all the works of Burns at hand, a preacher will find it profitable to read all the poet had to say on death and immortality such as his "Prayer in the Prospect of Death" and "Man Was Made to Mourn."

Other suitable poems for quotation at a funeral are —

"The Burial of the Dead"	— Keble
"The Death of an Infant"	— Milton
"Hymn for the Dead"	— Walter Scott
"Intimations of Immortality"	— Wordsworth
"The Reaper and the Flowers"	— Longfellow
"The Sleep"	— Elizabeth Browning
"Threnody"	— Emerson
"Adonais"	— Shelley

How true it is as Cabot and Dicks remind us in their chapter on "The Bereaved" in *The Art of Ministering to the Sick* that, "There is the accumulated wisdom of Scripture and poetry which like living friends can help us by contagion. Poets do not argue but assert conviction in expressive ways. What they see we can glimpse when we are stricken. In this the minister can help, especially if he knows bereavement by personal experience." Dr. Oswald Smith, of Toronto, was one who "sat where they sat" when in 1914 he wrote his poem on "Sorrow's Consolation" which appears in his volume, *Poems of a Lifetime*.

> Deep shadows fall, the night grows dark and dreary,
>   Cold breaks the day and all the world is sad;
> Under the sky the heavy clouds hang weary,
>   For death has torn away the best I had.

*   *   *

Similar in sentiment is the brief poem "Death" in Dr. James H. Hyslop's *Poems — Original and Translations*.

> It is not loneliness of soul,
> Nor grief nor tears that sternly bring
> The pall that rests on broken hearts,
> But shattered hopes and bleeding wounds
> Of mind and spirit, slow to heal.
> And gentle souls will ever weep
> When death's cold ruthless hand lays hold
> The silver cords of love and life.

*   *   *

Joseph F. Wagner issued, in 1899, a most profitable book called *God-Speed*, or "Well Wishing in Verse and Prose for All Occasions." Among its compositions for any event you can think of, a section is devoted to inscriptions for tombstones covering all ages and types of people. There are also *Elegies for Deaths and Burials — of a Minister and of a Teacher*. This is indeed a valuable handbook for a pastor to possess.

*   *   *

In *The Valley of Silence*, published by Zondervan Publishing House, Grand Rapids, there is a beautiful poem on "Should You Go First," the last verse of which reads —

> Should you go first and I remain,
>   One thing I'd have to do,

Walk slowly down the path of death,
  For soon I'll follow you.
I'll want to know each step you take,
  That I may walk the same.
For someday down that lonely road
  You'll hear me call your name.

As for appropriate funeral hymns, many of which we have already suggested, it is important for the pastor to have at hand a reliable book of hymnology. Julian's masterpiece, *Dictionary of Hymnology*, is useful not only for its biographical data regarding hymnists and poets, but also for the information it supplies of the background or history of several hymns, such as "Rock of Ages." The most recent work on this subject is *The Judson Concordance to Hymns* by McDormand T. B. and Crossland F., and published by Judson Press, Valley Forge, Pa. As hymns are an integral part of our Christian heritage, and furnish a pastor with appropriate homiletical illustration material, this hymnal concordance, listing 2342 hymns taken from 27 hymnbooks in common use among major denominations, supplies the best hymns available on death, burial and bereavement. How uplifting are some of the old favorites, such as —

"Sun of my soul, Thou Saviour dear."
"God moves in a mysterious way."
"Art thou weary, art thou languid."
"Jerusalem the Golden."
"There is a land of pure delight."
"My faith looks up to Thee."
"Forever with the Lord."
"When the mists have rolled in splendor."
"There is a calm beyond life's fitful fever."
"Still, still with Thee, when purple morning breaketh."
"The sands of time are sinking."
"Come let us join our friends above."
"Fade, fade, each earthly joy; Jesus is mine!"
"How bright these glorious spirits shine."
"For all the saints who from their labors rest."

Complete Poems

"AND HE CALLED A LITTLE CHILD"

Beyond the planets and the far-off stars
   Our little sister's ear heard God's clear call;
Life's sunny noon, its reddening sunset bars,
   And pleasant evening shades — she left them all.
So now "she never would know pain and sin" —
Such halting comfort we each other gave
When like a dove her soul had fluttered in
   High heaven's opening gate;
Yet standing by her waxen body in the grave
Endeavoring to quiet sorrow's din
   We wept — so desolate!

Lord, when the eternal summons comes for me
   To take the last lone stretch that ends life's day
Ere I the King in all His beauty see,
   With a rejoicing heart may I forget the way
So full of things I could not understand —
The griefs and dark crimes of a cruel world —
   And may I firmly hold with faithful hand,
If black the night and wild
The banner of Thy love aloft — unfurled,
That angels may when I before Thee stand
   Say, "He called a little child."
                —Grace W. Haight

*   *   *

O FOR A FAITH THAT WILL NOT SHRINK

O for a faith that will not shrink,
Though pressed by every foe
That will not tremble on the brink
Of any earthly woe!

That will not murmur or complain
Beneath the chastening rod,
But, in the hour of grief or pain,
Will lean upon its God.

A faith that shines more bright and clear
When tempests rage without,
That when in danger knows no fear,
In darkness feels no doubt;

Lord, give us such a faith as this,
And then, whate'er may come,
We'll taste e'en here the hallowed bliss
Of the eternal home.
                    —William H. Bathurst

* * *

THE WEAVER

My life is but a weaving
    Between my Lord and me;
I may not choose the colors,
    He knows what they should be;
For He can view the pattern
    Upon the upper side,
While I can see it only
    On this, the under side.

Sometimes He weaveth sorrow,
    Which seems strange to me;
But I will trust His judgment,
    And work as faithfully;
'Tis He who fills the shuttle,
    He knows just what is best,
So I shall weave in earnest
    And leave with Him the rest.

Not till the loom is silent
    And the shuttles cease to fly
Shall God unroll the canvas
    And explain the reason why—
The dark threads are as needful
    In the weaver's skillful hand
As the threads of gold and silver
    In the pattern He has planned.
                    —Anonymous

* * *

CROSSING THE BAR

Sunset and evening star,
    And one clear call for me!
And may there be no moaning of the bar,
    When I put out to sea,

But such a tide as moving seems asleep,
　Too full for sound and foam,
When that which drew from out the boundless deep
　Turns again home.

Twilight and evening bell,
　And after that the dark!
And may there be no sadness of farewell,
　When I embark;

For tho' from out our bourne of Time and Place
　The flood may bear me far,
I hope to see my Pilot face to face
　When I have crossed the bar.

—Alfred Tennyson

* * *

SOME TIME WE'LL UNDERSTAND

Not now, but in the coming years, It may be in the better land,
We'll read the meaning of our tears, And there, some time, we'll understand.

We'll catch the broken thread again, And finish what we here began;
Heav'n will the mysteries explain. And then, ah, then, we'll understand.

We'll know why clouds instead of sun Were over many a cherished plan;
Why song has ceased when scarce begun; 'Tis there, some time, we'll
understand.

God knows the way, He holds the key, He guides us with unerring hand;
Some time with tearless eyes we'll see; Yes, there, up there, we'll understand.

Then trust in God thro' all the days; Fear not, for He doth hold thy hand;
Though dark thy way, still sing and praise, Some time, some time, we'll
understand.

—Maxwell N. Cornelius

* * *

JERUSALEM THE GOLDEN

Jerusalem, the golden, With milk and honey blest!
Beneath thy contemplation Sink heart and voice oppressed;
I know not, O I know not What joys await me there;
What radiancy of glory, What bliss beyond compare.

They stand, those halls of Zion, All jubilant with song,
And bright with many an angel, And all the martyr throng,
The Prince is ever in them, The day-light is serene;
The pastures of the blessed Are decked in glorious sheen.

O sweet and blessed country, Shall I e'er see thy face?
O sweet and blessed country, Shall I e'er win thy grace?
Exult, O dust and ashes! The Lord shall be thy part;
His only, His forever, Thou shalt be, and thou art!

—Bernard of Cluny

* * *

SAFE IN THE ARMS OF JESUS

Safe in the arms of Jesus, Safe on His gentle breast,
There by His love o'ershaded, Sweetly my soul shall rest.
Hark! 'tis the voice of angels, Borne in a song to me,
Over the fields of glory, Over the jasper sea.

Safe in the arms of Jesus, Safe from corroding care,
Safe from the world's temptations, Sin cannot harm me there.
Free from the blight of sorrow, Free from my doubts and fears;
Only a few more trials, Only a few more tears!

Jesus, my heart's dear refuge, Jesus has died for me;
Firm on the Rock of Ages, Ever my trust shall be.
Here let me wait with patience, Wait till the night is o'er;
Wait till I see the morning Break on the golden shore.

Safe in the arms of Jesus, Safe on His gentle breast,
There by His love o'ershaded, Sweetly my soul shall rest.

—Fanny Crosby

* * *

JESUS, BLESSED JESUS

There's one who can comfort when all else fails,
Jesus, blessed Jesus;
A Saviour who saves tho' the foe assails,
Jesus, blessed Jesus:
Once He traveled the way we go, Felt the pangs of deceit and woe;
Who more perfectly then can know
Than Jesus, blessed Jesus?

He never forsakes in the darkest hour,
Jesus, blessed Jesus;
His arm is around us with keeping power,
Jesus, blessed Jesus:
When we enter the Shadowland, When at Jordan we trembling stand,
He will meet us with outstretched hand,
This Jesus, blessed Jesus.

What joy it will be when we see His face,
Jesus, blessed Jesus;
Forever to sing of His love and grace,

Jesus, blessed Jesus:
There at home on that shining shore, With the loved ones gone on before,
We will praise Him forever-more,
Our Jesus, blessed Jesus.

—Charles H. Gabriel

* * *

FADE, FADE, EACH EARTHLY JOY

Fade, fade, each earthly joy; Jesus is mine.
Break every tender tie; Jesus is mine.
Dark is the wilderness, Earth has no resting-place,
Jesus alone can bless; Jesus is mine.

Tempt not my soul away; Jesus is mine.
Here would I ever stay; Jesus is mine.
Perishing things of clay, Born but for one brief day,
Pass from my heart away; Jesus is mine.

Farewell, ye dreams of night; Jesus is mine.
Lost in this dawning bright, Jesus is mine.
All that my soul has tried Left but a dismal void;
Jesus has satisfied; Jesus is mine.

Farewell, mortality; Jesus is mine.
Welcome, eternity; Jesus is mine.
Welcome, O loved and blest, Welcome, sweet scenes of rest,
Welcome, my Saviour's breast; Jesus is mine.

—Jane C. Bonar

* * *

COME, YE DISCONSOLATE

Come, ye disconsolate, where'er ye languish,
Come to the mercy-seat, fervently kneel;
Here bring your wounded hearts, here tell your anguish;
Earth has no sorrows that heaven cannot heal.

Joy of the desolate, light of the straying,
Hope of the penitent, fadeless and pure!
Here speaks the Comforter, in mercy saying,
"Earth has no sorrows that heaven cannot cure."

Here see the bread of life; see waters flowing
Forth from the throne of God, pure from above.
Come to the feast prepared; come, ever knowing
Earth has no sorrows but heaven can remove.

—Thomas Moore

* * *

RESIGNATION

There is no death! What seems so is transition.
  This life of mortal breath
Is but a suburb of the life elysian,
  Whose portal we call Death.

She is not dead — the child of our affection,
  But gone unto that school
Where she no longer needs our poor protection,
  And Christ Himself doth rule.

In that great cloister's stillness and seclusion,
  By guardian angels led,
Safe from temptation, safe from sin's pollution.
  She lives, whom we call dead.

Day after day we think what she is doing
  In those bright realms of air;
Year after year her tender steps pursuing,
  Behold her grown more fair.

Thus do we walk with her, and keep unbroken
  The bond which nature gives,
Thinking that our remembrance, though unspoken,
  May reach her where she lives.

Not as a child shall we again behold her;
  For when with raptures wild
In our embraces we again enfold her,
  She will not be a child.

But a fair maiden, in her Father's mansion,
  Clothed with celestial grace;
And beautiful with all the soul's expansion,
  Shall we behold her face.
              —Henry Wadsworth Longfellow

*   *   *

THERE IS NO SORROW, LORD, TOO LIGHT

  There is no sorrow, Lord, too light
  To bring in prayer to Thee;
  There is no anxious care too slight
  To wake Thy sympathy.

  Thou, who hast trod the thorny road,
  Wilt share each small distress;
  The love which bore the greater load
  Will not refuse the less.

There is no secret sigh we breathe
But meets Thine ear divine;
And every cross grows light beneath
The shadow, Lord, of Thine.

—Jane Crewdson

* * *

SHOULD YOU GO FIRST

Should you go first and I remain
  To walk the road alone,
I'll live in memory's garden, dear,
  With happy days we've known.
In spring I'll wait for roses red
  When fade the lilacs blue;
In early fall when brown leaves fall,
  I'll catch a glimpse of you.

Should you go first and I remain
  For battles to be fought,
Each thing you've touched along the way
  Will be a hallowed spot.
I'll hear your voice, I'll see your smile,
  Though blindly I may grope,
The memory of your helping hand
  Will buoy me with hope.

Should you go first and I remain
  To finish with the scroll,
No lengthening shadows shall creep in
  To make this life seem droll.
We've known so much of happiness,
  We've had our cup of joy.
And memory is one gift of God
  That death cannot destroy.

Should you go first and I remain,
  One thing I'd have to do,
Walk slowly down the path of death,
  For soon I'll follow you.
I'll want to know each step you take,
  That I may walk the same.
For someday down that lonely road
  You'll hear me call your name.

—Albert Rowswell

* * *

HOW BLEST THE RIGHTEOUS WHEN HE DIES

How blest the righteous when he dies!
When sinks a weary soul to rest!
How mildly beam the closing eyes!
How gently heaves the expiring breast!

So fades a summer cloud away;
So sinks the gale when storms are o'er;
So gently shuts the eyes of day;
So dies the wave along the shore.

A holy quiet reigns around,
A calm which life not death destroys;
And naught disturbs the peace profound
Which his unfettered soul enjoys.

Life's labor done, as sinks the clay,
Light from its load the spirit flies,
While heav'n and earth combine to say,
"How blest the righteous when he dies."
—Barbauld

* * *

IT IS NOT DEATH TO DIE

It is not death to die,
To leave this weary road,
And midst the brotherhood on high
To be at home with God.

It is not death to close
The eye long dimmed by tears,
And wake in glorious repose
To spend eternal years.

It is not death to bear
The stroke that sets us free
From earthly chain, to breathe the air
Of boundless liberty.

It is not death to fling
Aside this mortal dust,
And rise on strong exulting wing
To live among the just.

Giver and Lord of life!
In thee we cannot die;
Grant us to conquer in the strife,
And dwell with thee on high.
—H. A. Cesar Malan

HOUSE OF MANY MANSIONS

In the house of many mansions
Christ my Lord prepares a place,
Where His own — all His own —
Shall dwell in the light of His face.

In the house of many mansions
Neither toil nor care shall come;
But His own — all His own —
Forever shall rest in that home.

In that house of many mansions
Death shall nevermore molest;
But His own — all His own —
Shall be by their Lord fully blest.

Mansions — O house of many mansions
Prepared in heav'n for me;
Mansions — O house of many mansions . . .
Where I shall dwell, where I shall dwell
    with Thee.

Copyright 1935 by Geo. S. Schuler in *Pastor Ironside's Gospel Songs*.
Assigned to Singspiration, Inc.

* * *

HOME!

At the close of a busy anxious day,
    As our thoughts toward home we turn,
How our spirits thrill, as we wend our way.
    And for welcome rest we yearn!
But what will it be when we come at last
    To the gates of our home on high,
When the final hour of toil is past
    And eternal rest is nigh?

How we long for the loved ones waiting us,
    When afar we've chanced to roam!
How our pulses quicken as on we press
    To their eager "welcome home"!
But what will it be when we catch a glimpse
    Of our heavenly abode,
Where those who have entered in long since,
    Await in that land of love?

And what will it be, when our eyes behold
    The Lamb on His kingly throne,
When He welcomes us to the heavenly fold,
    And the joy of His Father's home?

As we bow at His blessed nail-pierced feet,
  To worship and to adore,
Ah, that will be ecstasy full, complete,
  Abiding forevermore!

Then let us with patience carry on
  To the end of our pilgrim way,
For glory waits at the setting sun,
  And joy at the close of day:
And the Saviour stands at the gates àjar,
  With His arms outstretched in love,
To welcome His own, who have journeyed far,
  To the warmth of His home above.

Copyright by Loizeaux Brothers, Inc. Assigned to Singspiration, Inc.

* * *

WHAT GOD HATH PROMISED

God hath not promised
  Skies always blue,
Flower-strewn pathways
  All our lives through;
God hath not promised
  Sun without rain,
Joy without sorrow,
  Peace without pain.

But God hath promised
  Strength for the day,
Rest for the labor,
  Light for the way,
Grace for the trials,
  Help from above,
Unfailing sympathy,
  Undying love.

—Annie Johnson Flint
Used by permission of Evangelical Publishers

* * *

Organ Preludes and Postludes
"O God, Our Help in Ages Past"
"The King of Love My Shepherd Is"
"Lead, Kindly Light"
"Consolation" (Mendelssohn)
"I Need Thee Every Hour"
"Safe in the Arms of Jesus"
"In the Hour of Trial"
"Be Still My Soul" (Finlandia)
"When Thou Art Near" (Bach)

"Jesus, Still Lead On"
"What a Friend We Have in Jesus"
"O Sacred Head Now Wounded"
"Come, Thou Fount of Every Blessing"
"When I Survey the Wondrous Cross"
"Beneath the Cross of Jesus"
"Guide Me O Thou Great Jehovah"
"Wonderful Peace"
"Nearer My God to Thee"
"Abide With Me"
"Still, Still With Thee"
"Come, Sweet Repose" (Bach)
"The Funeral March" (Chopin)
"My Heart Is Filled With Longing" (Bach)
"My Faith Looks Up To Thee"
"Hark, Hark, My Soul"
"Largo" (Handel)
"Oh, Rest in the Lord" (Mendelssohn)
"Ten Thousand Times Ten Thousand"
"I Know That My Redeemer Liveth" (Handel)
"Blest Be the Tie"
"Rock of Ages"
"Peace, Perfect Peace"
"One Sweetly Solemn Thought"
"For All the Saints"
"Jerusalem, the Golden"
"Jesus, Lover of My Soul"
"Now Let Every Tongue Adore Thee"

* * *

Of Scripture Selections

Already, in our suggestions for various kinds of burials, we have indicated appropriate selections from Scripture to be read or preached upon, and as there is no other book comparable to God's Word for comfort and hope, a pastor should hide within his heart as many of its comfortable words as possible. Phrases like, "Blessed are they that mourn for they shall be comforted," "The God of all comfort," "Comforted of God," will never be outworn or superceded. *The Scripture Sourcebook*, published by Zondervan's, Grand Rapids, is most helpful in that it arranges references around a given subject. Thus, if themes like death, sorrow, comfort and heaven are to be dealt with, a pastor will find ample material to work upon.

Another help is that of one of the many books on "Daily

Portions," such as *The Christian's Daily Companion* in which hundreds of promises are classified. Under *death* or *resurrection* or *heaven*, etc., suitable Scriptures are given and at the foot of each list is a fitting verse of poetry. *All the Promises of the Bible*, by the writer, and published by Zondervan's, might also act as a guidepost in the preparation of messages for burials and the bereaved. No matter what occasion may arise, God's infallible Word can supply the necessary direction. The pastor might appreciate to have a list of Biblical benedictions before him. Here are the most conspicuous among them —

The Lord bless thee, and keep thee:
The Lord make his face shine upon thee, and be gracious unto thee:
The Lord lift up his countenance upon thee and give thee peace. *Numbers 6:24-26*

* * *

To God only wise, be glory through Jesus Christ forever. Amen. *Romans 16:27*

* * *

Grace be unto you, and peace, from God our Father, and from the Lord Jesus Christ. *1 Corinthians 1:3*

* * *

The grace of our Lord Jesus Christ, and the love of God, and the communion of the Holy Ghost, be with you all. Amen. *1 Corinthians 13:14*

* * *

Brethren, the grace of our Lord Jesus Christ be with your spirit. Amen. *Galatians 6:18*

* * *

Peace be to the brethren, and love with faith, from God the Father and the Lord Jesus Christ. Grace be with all them that love our Lord Jesus Christ in sincerity. Amen.
Ephesians 6:23, 24

* * *

The peace of God, which passeth all understanding, shall keep your hearts and minds through Christ Jesus. Now unto God and our Father be glory for ever and ever. Amen.
Philippians 4:7, 20

Grace, mercy and peace, from God the Father and Jesus
Christ our Lord.   *I Timothy 1:2*

* * *

Grace unto you, and peace, from God our Father and the
Lord Jesus Christ.   *II Thessalonians 1:2*

* * *

Now the God of peace, that brought again from the dead
our Lord Jesus, that great Shepherd of the sheep, through
the blood of the everlasting covenant, Make you perfect in
every good work to do his will, working in you that which
is wellpleasing in his sight, through Jesus Christ; to whom
be glory for ever and ever. Amen.   *Hebrews 13:20, 21*

* * *

Grace and peace be multiplied unto you through the
knowledge of God, and of Jesus Christ our Lord.
II Peter 1:2

* * *

Grace be with you, mercy and peace, from God the
Father, and from the Lord Jesus Christ, the Son of the
Father, in truth and love.   *II John 3*

* * *

Now unto him that is able to keep you from falling, and
to present you faultless before the presence of his glory with
exceeding joy, To the only wise God our Saviour, be glory
and majesty, dominion and power, both now and ever.
Amen.   *Jude 24, 25*

* * *

The grace of our Lord Jesus Christ be with you all. Amen.
Revelation 22:21

* * *

Of Suitable Quotations

While there are several volumes of quotations, sayings and
proverbs on the market, and a pastor should have one or two of
the best in his library, he will find that his own gathered grain
may provide him with apt gems of truth he can weave into any
necessary message. A small indexed note book should ever be on

hand to make prisoner of all the good sayings he hears or reads. Often a thought or phrase of truth is resident in a quotation which the preacher can profitably expand. For material relevant to funeral services some of the following pregnant sentences may be of service.

"Fear not death; for the sooner we die, the longer shall we be immortal."

* * *

"As soon as we are born, we commence our pilgrimage to the grave."

* * *

"When you must go, then go, And make as little fuss as you can" —*Tao Chien.*

* * *

"How strange this fear of death is, yet we are never frightened at a sunset" —*George Macdonald.*

* * *

"That fatal sergeant, *Death,* spares no degree" —*Stirling.*

* * *

"Every door may be shut but Death's door."

* * *

"Death and dice level all distinction" —*Samuel Foote.*

* * *

"In every parting, there is an image of Death" —*George Eliot.*

* * *

"Death moulded into calm completeness the status of his life" —*Whittier.*

* * *

"One step to the deathbed, and one to the bier,
And one to the charnel, and one — O where?"

* * *

"Remain as noble and good as you have been in the past. This is the last wish of your dying father" —*Frederick IV,* to his daughter.

* * *

"I thank God I have always carried this in my mind, that

nothing was left to the last hour" —Last word of *Queen Mary*, of Orange.

* * *

"It is beautiful to die in this house, where the king has paid a visit" —Last word of *Talleyrand* as Louis Philippe left the room.

* * *

"Death is the great key that opens the gate of Eternity" —*Milton*.

* * *

"There is no Death; What seems so is transition" —*Long-fellow*.

* * *

"I go with the gladness of a boy bounding away from school. I feel so strong in Christ" —Last word of *Adoniram Judson*.

* * *

"I shall be satisfied — satisfied — satisfied, when I awake in Thy likeness!" —*Charles Wesley's* farewell word.

* * *

"I cannot think of death as more than the going out of one room into another" —*William Blake*.

* * *

"Going out into life — that is dying" —*Henry Ward Beecher*.

* * *

"Ah, is this dying? How I have dreaded as an enemy this smiling friend!" —*James Goodwin* as he died.

* * *

"The Lord teach you to die" —*Richard Baxter's* last word to a fellow-pastor.

* * *

"It is my highest ambition to go from Blackfriars to heaven" —Puritan *William Gouge's* wish was fulfilled.

* * *

"When I arrive at the world of blessedness, I shall shout, Grace, Grace!" —*Isaac Toms*.

* * *

* * *

"The labors of this mortal life end in a large reward."
* * *

"Death is much sweeter to me with the testimony of truth than life with the least denial" —*Geleazium* at his martyrdom.
* * *

"There is no place where earth's sorrows are more felt, Than up in heaven."
* * *

"Here is the broken casket, but God has in His own keeping the invisible gem — the soul" —*A. H. DeLong*.
* * *

"Give me no guess for the dying pillow" —*Joseph Cook*.
* * *

"God's finger touched him and he slept" —*Tennyson*.
* * *

"Heaven is above all yet: there sits a Judge That no king can corrupt" —*Shakespeare*.
* * *

"Heaven's eternal year is thine" —*Dryden*.
* * *

Of Famous Last Sayings

A further aid for the pastor when called upon to care for the dying, bury the dead and comfort the living is a collection of the dying moments and messages of distinguished men and women. Literature on "Last Sayings" is not too hard to find. In the writer's own work, *The Art of Dying* — an anthology of famous last words, a list has been enumerated. Such a fascinating study confirms the sentiment Shakespeare expresses that —

> The tongues of dying men
> Enforce attention like deep harmony;
> Where words are scarce they're seldom spent in vain,
> For they breathe truth that breathe their words in pain.

Because of his association with the dying, the pastor may find that their end and final message correspond to the experiences of saints of old. Recounting some of these records can bring comfort to those whose end is that of peace. Incidentally, the pastor may find in a volume or two of collected "last sayings" some interesting material for a few sermons on such a theme. We herewith cite several by way of example —

John Quincy Adams, sixth President of the U. S. A. (1767-1848), was stricken with paralysis on February 21st, 1848, and died two days later. His last words were —

"It is the last of earth! I am content!"
How happy is the person who leaves earth content in Christ!

* * *

Joseph Addison (1672-1719), the renowned poet and essayist, called his relative, the young, dissolute Lord Warwick to his death bed and said to him —

"See in what peace a Christian can die?"

* * *

Roche de Bailli (1605), a distinguished French physician uttered these words as he died —

"I must now hasten away since my baggage has been sent on before me."

* * *

Pope John XXIII, just before his death in 1962, said to his physician, Gasparrine —

"Dear professor, don't be disturbed. My bags are always packed so when the moment to depart arrives, I won't lose any time."

* * *

Howard Crosby (1826-1891), the well-known Presbyterian minister and Chancellor of the University of New York, left this testimony as he died —

"My heart is resting sweetly with Jesus, and my hand is in his."

* * *

William Cullen (1712-1790), a famous physician of his time, met death just as calmly —

"I wish I had the power of writing, for then I would describe to you how pleasant a thing it is to die."

* * *

Samuel Hopkins (1721-1803), conspicuous theologian died in faith saying —

"My anchor is well cast, and my ship, though weather-beaten, will outride the storm."

* * *

Julian (331-363), the Roman Emperor, known as "The Apostate" because of his renunciation of Christianity, died with the confession on his lips —

"Thou hast conquered, O Galilean! Thou hast conquered!"

* * *

Hugh Latimer (1472-1555), the English reformer and martyr said to Ridley, his companion at the stake —

"Be of good comfort, Master Ridley, and play the man. We shall this day light such a candle by God's grace in England, as I trust shall never be put out."

* * *

Mary, Countess of Warwick (1678), who is credited with the famous question, "Why are we so fond of that life which begins with a cry, and ends with a groan?" was certain of the larger life beyond the grave —

"Well, ladies, if I were one hour in heaven, I would not be again with you, as much as I love you."

* * *

Cotton Mather (1633-1728), one of the most remarkable men in the early religious life of America, said to his wife as she wiped his eyes with her handkerchief —

"I am going where all tears will be wiped away."

* * *

Philipp Melanchthon (1497-1568), the close friend of Martin Luther, replied to a friend at his deathbed if he wanted anything further —

"Nothing else but heaven."

* * *

Richard Newton (1676-1753), the English divine who founded Hertford College, Oxford, died triumphantly saying —

"Christ Jesus the Saviour of sinners and life of the dead. I am going, going to Glory! Farewell sin! Farewell Death! Praise the Lord!"

* * *

John Preston (1587-1628), author of "Treatise on the Covenant" died saying —

"Blessed be God, though I change my place, I shall not change my company; for I have walked with God while living, and now I go to rest with God."

* * *

Charles Reade (1814-1884), the renowned novelist had Paul's record of his translation to Paradise (II Corinthians 12:1-4) in mind as he died uttering —

"Amazing, amazing Glory! I am having Paul's understanding."

* * *

Samuel Rutherford (1695-1779), that seraphic soul whose *Letters* are a spiritual classic, had a glorious end —

"If He should slay me ten thousand times, ten thousand times I'll trust Him. I feel, I feel, I believe in joy, and rejoice; I feed on manna. O for arms to embrace Him! O for a well-tuned harp!"

* * *

Robert Sanderson (1587-1663), Bishop of London and chaplain to Charles I, died in assurance exclaiming —

"My heart is fixed O God! my heart is fixed, where true joy is to be found."

* * *

Henry Timrod (1829-1867), American poet, who, finding that he could no longer swallow water, said —

"Never mind, I shall soon drink of the river of eternal life."

John Wesley (1703-1791), founder of Methodism, surrounded by many of his chief leaders as he lay dying, murmured —

"The best of all is God is with us."

* * *

Sarah Wesley, wife of Charles Wesley, John's brother, died asking —

"Open the gates! Open the gates!"

* * *

Zeno, (about 355 B.C.), Greek Philosopher and founder of the Stoics, had this to say at the end —

"Earth, dost thou demand me? I am ready."

* * *

We could go on ad infinitum, but trust we have whetted the appetite for a most substantial meal of this kind. The pastor will find in the "last sayings" especially those of many of the martyrs and convenanters, in works like Fox's *Book of Martyrs* and *Last Days of Eminent Christians* by Andrew Bonar, much interesting material to draw upon in the preparation of a funeral message, and in letters he may write to the bereaved relatives of those he had to bury. For instance, a warm, sympathetic letter to a bereaved mother and her family as soon as the bread-winner had been taken can come as "the oil of joy for mourning." The pastor, writing on behalf of the church of which the deceased was a member and possibly a loyal worker, could include a farewell saying in this way —

Dear sorrowing Friends,

It is hard to express oneself at a time like this. All of us in the fellowship of the church which your dear one deeply loved, wish me to say that they are all prayerfully remembering you in your grief. While you have lost one who was so precious to your hearts, the fellow members of the church mourn with you for they have said "Farewell!" to one they held in high regard as one of Christ's loyal followers. Now, as the renowned preacher, Samuel Hopkins, confessed as he died, "My anchor is well cast, and my ship, though weather-beaten, will outride the storm," your beloved one had an anchor well-cast in Christ, and has outridden the storm of death, and is now with Christ which is far better. May the Lord make His consolations to abound on your behalf, and cause you to know that He is perfecting that which concerns both you and yours! God bless you!

Of Effective Illustrations

Because the purpose of an illustration or story is the stirring of the imagination of hearers, such an element should not be lacking in a sermon. Jesus expressed Himself through many illustrations of various forms. The long list of His word-pictures prove Him to be an illustrator of truth. In His Sermon on the Mount, as given by Matthew, Jesus used at least sixty-two figures of speech. His illustrations can be found on almost every page of the gospels, and in every case they were used to illuminate the glory of the truth presented. He never told a story for the sake of telling it — as some preachers do as mere padding. His pictures were always relevant to the message of the moment, and the experience of many a pastor confirms the truth of Macaulay's statement that "Logicians may reason about abstractions, but the great mass of men must have images." Imagery in a sermon clothes the message in moments when "it rises above the ground line of familiar facts and is inflamed with passion or exalted by thought," as Emerson puts it.

In a funeral sermon, illustrations should be apt, brief and of a consoling nature. Here are a few from which a preacher can draw.

When Robert Ingersoll, the famed agnostic died, the printed notice of his funeral service read, "There will be no singing." He died without learning to sing the new song of Moses and the Lamb. How songless and joyless are sin and unbelief!

C. S. Lewis, in his book, *A Grief Observed*, gives us a series of reflections when his much-loved wife died. Describing her last moments he wrote, "How wicked it would be, if we could, to call the dead back! She said, not to me but to the chaplain, 'I am at

peace with God.' She smiled but not at me. *Poi si torno all'
eierna fontana.*"

Dr. A. C. Dixon, the outstanding evangelist pastor of a past
decade, who was pastor of Spurgeon's Tabernacle, London, for
a while, tells a touching story of his own family circle in the
volume *The Bright Side of Life*. On the Christmas morning after
the death of the eldest child, all sat at the breakfast table, much
too silent for Christmas Day. Silence was broken, however, by
one of the children saying, "This is Howard's first Christmas in
heaven, isn't it?" Mother Dixon replied, "I would like to know
if it is not Christmas *every* day in heaven." Do not our blessed
dead have a Christmas every day in heaven, seeing that the
unseen host ever remember in the glory land, the Saviour's con-
descension, love, sacrifice and grace? Over there, the glorified
never cease singing praises to the Lamb who was slain, but who
is alive for evermore.

Dr. George C. Robinson, one-time Professor of Old Testament,
McCormick Theological Seminary, once remarked — "Most people dread death, but personally, I am not afraid to die, though
I don't court death . . . Christians face death with faith, believing
that it opens the door 'to a land of goodness and gladness . . .'
Sudden death means sudden glory. Think of the thrill the
believer will feel upon arriving home."

> Think of stepping on shore,
> And finding it heaven!
> Think of taking hold of a hand,
> And finding it God's hand!
> Think of breathing a new air
> And finding it celestial air!
> Of feeling invigorated,
> And finding it immortality!
> Of passing from storm and tempest into perfect calm!
> Of awaking and knowing—
>   I am home!

When Frederick Denison Maurice, the renowned preacher
came to die, a friend said to him, "Well, you have preached
your last sermon." "Aye," Maurice replied, "but only my last
sermon in *this* life." John Newton, who gave us "Amazing grace,
how sweet the sound," said as he neared the end, "I am still in

the land of the dying: I shall be in the land of the living soon." What expansion of all our powers eternity holds for us!

Graven on the tombstone of Charles Kingsley and his much-loved wife are the three Latin words, *Amavimus, Amamus, Amabimus*, "We have loved, we love, we shall love." Heaven is not a sphere of ethereal, cold, unsocial and formless spirits but a home of saints with glorified bodies having a perpetual inter-change of perfect love and affection. Love, redeemed from all grossness and sensuality is to be our portion forever. We shall know and love each other better when the mists have rolled away.

Francis of Assisi (1183-1225), founder of the Franciscan Order of Monks, had a passionate love of nature, and spoke of the birds as little brothers and sisters. One day, while hoeing his garden, he was asked what he would do if he were suddenly to learn that he was to die at sunset that day. His reply was, "I would finish hoeing my garden."

* * *

Stephen Girard (1750-1831), French-born, American philan-thropist, had a similar idea in mind when he said, "When death comes to me it will find me busy, unless I am asleep. If I thought I was going to die tomorrow, I should nevertheless plant a tree today."

* * *

Benjamin Franklin (1706-1790), a man of many parts, was the statesman who had a share in the drafting of the American Declaration of Independence. He it was who said, "Death takes no bribes," and he also wrote, "If you would not be forgotten as soon as you are dead, either write things worth reading, or do things worth writing." At the end of his fascinating career he whispered as he died, "A dying man can do nothing easy."

* * *

Abraham Lincoln (1809-1865), sixteenth President of the U. S., and slave emancipator, had no idea he was to be cruelly assas-sinated when he gave utterance to the sentiment, "Die when I may, I want it said of me by those who knew me best, that I always plucked a thistle and planted a flower where I thought a flower would grow." Such a noble ambition was often realized by Lincoln in the course of his pilgrimage.

In that absorbing book, *The Legends of the Rhine,* there is a story bearing the title, "The Bells of Speyer," which tells of the passing of a great and kindly emperor. It was believed that, "Just at the moment of his death the bells in the cathedral at Speyer tolled without any human hand putting them in motion, as they always did when an imperial death took place." William L. Stidger in his book of poems, *I Saw God Wash the World,* made this legend the basis of a fascinating poem on the death of Christ, he called "The Death Imperial." Its first verse reads —

> His was the Death Imperial:
> The lightning flash, the earthquake roll,
> The moan of a majestic soul;
> A great reverberant, reverent toll,
> A crash of thunder through the earth,
> A triumph of eternal worth;
> The temple veil asunder rent,
> The sacrifice, magnificent!

The Cathedral of Milan has three doorways and over each arch is an impressive inscription. Over one great arch are the words, *All that pleases is but for a moment.* Over another arch is the sentence, *All that troubles is but for a moment.* But, over the central arch are these significant words, *That only is important which is eternal.* How essential it is to keep eternal values in view! What is our brief span on earth in comparison with the unending eternity before us!

William Cuthill, the Scottish seaman, was one of those brave covenanters who willingly died for his Lord. Accused of being associated with those who murdered the evil primate, he was found guilty and executed, July 27, 1681. Before his death he affirmed —

> "I am ready to step into eternity as one of the subjects of a kingdom covenanted to God, and as one of Christ's sufferers . . . I adhere to all the faithful testimonies for truth in Scotland . . . Now, farewell world and all things in it. Welcome Lord Jesus Christ, into Thy hands I recommend my spirit."

John Sheppard, of whom little is known save that he was a godly pastor and most fruitful in his ministry, remarked to a few fellow-pastors who had gathered in his death-chamber —

> "The secret of my success is in these three things: the studying of my sermons frequently cost me tears. Before I preached a sermon to others, I derived good from it. I have gone into the pulpit as if I were immediately after to render an account to my Master."

* * *

William Shakespeare revealed his faith in God and in immortality in his *Last Will and Testament* signed in March, 1616. The first paragraph of this historic document reads —

> "I commend my soul into the hands of God my Creator, hoping and assuredly believing, through the only merits of Jesus Christ my Saviour, to be made partaker of life everlasting; my body to the earth, whereof it is made."

* * *

Socrates, the famous Athenian preacher and philosopher, believed in an after life. Condemned to die, as he came to drain the poisoned cup he exclaimed — "If the common expression be true that death conveys us to the place of departed men, with delight I drink this hemlock, for it sends my spirit to commune with Ajax and Palamedes." When asked by his disciples where he wished to be buried, he replied in words that became immortal —

> "Bury *me*, if you can catch *me*."

SUPPLEMENTARY READINGS

Bonar, Andrew *Last Days of Eminent Christians*

Cabot and Dicks *The Art of Ministering to the Sick* (Macmillan and Co., New York)

Forbush, W. B. (ed.) *Foxe's Book of Martyrs* (Zondervan, Grand Rapids) 1926

Fox, Selina F. *A Chain of Prayer Across the Ages*, (Dutton, New York)

Julian, John *Dictionary of Hymnology* (Dover, New York) 1907

Lewis, C. S. *A Grief Observed* (Faber and Faber, London)

Lockyer, Herbert *The Art of Dying* (Kregels, Grand Rapids) 1966

―――――――――― *All the Promises of the Bible* (Zondervan, Grand Rapids) 1962

Marshall, Catherine *A Man Called Peter* (McGraw-Hill, New York) 1951

McDormand, T. B. and Crossland, F. *Judson Concordance to Hymns* (Judson Press, Valley Forge, Pa.) 1965

Schuler, Jack (comp.) *The Valley of Silence* (Zondervan, Grand Rapids) 1956

Smith, Dr. Oswald *Poems of a Lifetime* (Christian Literature Crusade, Fort Washington, Pa.) 1962

Smyth, J. Patterson *The Gospel of the Hereafter* (Hodder and Stoughton, London) 1906

Stidger, William L. *I Saw God Wash the World* (Rodeheaver-Hall Mack Co., Philadelphia) 1934

Torrey, Reuben A. *The Scripture Sourcebook* (Zondervan, Grand Rapids)

Wagner, Joseph *God-speed* (Roxbury Publishing Co., New York) 1899

RECORD OF FUNERALS CONDUCTED

DATE	NAME	AGE	PLACE	SERMON	TEXT

RECORD OF FUNERALS CONDUCTED

DATE	NAME	AGE	PLACE	SERMON	TEXT

RECORD OF FUNERALS CONDUCTED

DATE	NAME	AGE	PLACE	SERMON	TEXT

RECORD OF FUNERALS
CONDUCTED

DATE	NAME	AGE	PLACE	SERMON	TEXT

RECORD OF FUNERALS
CONDUCTED

DATE	NAME	AGE	PLACE	SERMON	TEXT